D1726397

Twenty-year-old BC Crothers became a Christian while reading the New Testament at a private retreat in a German hotel. Thankfully, her questions and textual conflicts did not deter her from becoming a student of the Holy Bible. After joining the American Episcopal Church, she graduated from the three-year Education for Ministry program. She taught Sunday school classes from grade school to adults and became a biblical spiritual director. After writing and teaching from her workbooks, at the encouragement of her bishop, BC attended the Virginia Theological Seminary, earning a Master in Theological Studies degree. She has held most church positions while writing on Faith issues.

As a lover of God, family, friends, country, democracy, and the educational process throughout life, BC has always been intrigued by people's spiritual journeys. Her primary objective is to help people find strength in Faith through her writings. In this regard, she has authored *Art of Loving God*, and *Church-Filling Techniques for Building Community*, both books long out of print. The *What Jesus Heard-Biblical Hebrew for the Bible Reader* will undergo revision, but this project is on hold until the current research and writing schedule eases. BC, helping others in the writing field, is the previous owner of Soul Care Books, LLC.

BC presently lives in Florida with her husband, Jack, who serves as 'reader', bringing light to needed terms. You can reach out to her at bc.crothers@gmail.com or visit her website BCCrothersAuthor.com.

BC has two mottos she lives by:

Living is for Now.
Eternity is Forever.
Power is in the Pen.
Supreme Power is in the Sharing.

BC Crothers

The Lord's Prayer – Tidbits from Its Extraordinary History

AUSTIN MACAULEY PUBLISHERS™

LONDON • CAMBRIDGE • NEW YORK • SHARJAH

Ordering Information
Quantity sales: Special discounts are available on quantity purchases by corporations, associations, and others. For details, contact the publisher at the address below.

Publisher's Cataloging-in-Publication data
Crothers, BC
The Lord's Prayer – Tidbits from Its Extraordinary History

ISBN 9781649797513 (Paperback)
ISBN 9781649797520 (Hardback)
ISBN 9781649797544 (ePub e-book)
ISBN 9781649797537 (Audiobook)

Library of Congress Control Number: 2022903138

www.austinmacauley.com/us

First Published 2022
Austin Macauley Publishers LLC
40 Wall Street,33rd Floor, Suite 3302
New York, NY 10005
USA

mail-usa@austinmacauley.com
+1 (646) 5125767

All persons who contributed to the 1992 and 1998 workbooks are named in the book's Preface.

All persons who contributed to the writing of this book are mentioned in the book's Introduction.

Table of Contents

Preface

Written in 1992, *Bits of Interesting History about the Lord's Prayer* became a supplemental reading to *The Lord's Prayer* adult and teen workbooks. While teaching from the adult workbook in my church, '*Bits of…*' never saw the light of day due to time restraints. Every eighteen months or so, I dusted its cover and reread the work. Six, seven years later, I found the book dry; too intellectual and not enough heart. After its revision, the short book became a companion reading to *The Lord's Prayer Workbook*.

This time, I taught from the workbook in our diocesan churches. Early on, our new bishop heard of the classes and requested a copy. After reading *The Lord's Prayer Workbook* and its *Bits of Interesting History*, our bishop wrote a letter of recommendation to be included in its publication. Of course, as its author, I was thrilled.

However, the bishop threw me a curve by saying, "Get thee to a seminary." Not surprisingly, these decades later, I can still smile over his statement, for I know he was kindly stating his belief that a deeper theological understanding would benefit the book's writing and all future endeavors. He was so firm in his conviction that, for the first time in its history, the diocese contributed financially for me, a member of the laity, to attend seminary. I hope that this second revised writing will please the bishop. He was right. Education did deepen the core of my spiritual being and theological understanding.

Now, in 2020, I return to one of my first loves in writing. *The Lord's Prayer* has already been a precious gift as hundreds of thousands of books and articles have cascaded words to sing of its glory. But they never quite reached the mark. This contribution will also fall short, for no written word can ever capture *in toto* the prayer's depth of spiritual completeness. Yet, my hope remains that understanding the reasoning behind this historical offering will bring us closer to the awe our Lord's Prayer inspires and deserves—in the same way that we understand that Jesus lives among us in the here and now, guiding and answering prayer.

The Jewish people and the Hebrew religion provide the background for Jesus's prayer, for they were His people and His Faith. First-century Palestine provides the perimeter of Jesus's environment. In the first segment, The Jewish Heritage of Jesus, acknowledges that civilization-wise, it was a religiously favorable time for Jesus's ministry. First, travel had never been more accessible. Second, for the first time, universal laws connected countries. Third, the Jewish sects of Sadducees, Doctors of Law (Scribes), Pharisees, the Essenes, and Zealots, along with the schools of the Shammaites and the Hillelites, had ongoing religious and societal conflicting issues. The freedom for average Jewish citizens to debate in synagogues led to exchange of ideas and complaints that had never before been publicly verbalized. In this environment of stratification, newfound freedom emerged despite sect differences and strict adherence to their rules.

This writing does not include in-depth social ramifications or political discussions. Its scope, by necessity, is narrow: the birth of a new religion. It is a given that first-century 'advanced civilization' played its parts in shaping the changes that occurred in the Jewish religion and the birth of the Christian religion. Faith is alive, like the Holy Spirit, a personified entity.

The largest segment of this book belongs to the Historical Significance of the Lord's Prayer. It traces the prayer's phrases from the Old Testament and ancient Jewish prayers. It studies the prayers' inclusion in the New Testament and shows how the Primitive Church treated the Lord's Prayer.

The people who were with me in the beginning of this book's writing endeavor: the priests, bishop, a Jewish rabbi, friends, and staunch-supporter husband, deserve more than the simple phrase of thank you. It is with sorrow that some names are included posthumously, as they did not live long enough to see their shared knowledge and inspirations in print. The priests and staff of The Cathedral Church of Saint Peter in Saint Petersburg, Florida, offered an invaluable support system. This list certainly includes Rev. Canon William A. Bosbyshell, Rev. Walter W. Cawthorne, Rev. Joseph Diaz, Rev. Barry Howe, Rev. Canon James F. Kelly, and Rev. John W. Thomas. Each was gracious in giving their time to read, answer questions, and comment on various paragraphs. Logan Hurst served as my first editor and most stalwart supporter. I also wish to thank Ida F. Davidoff, Ph.D., Charles J. Hirsch, M.D., Rabbi Jacob Luski, Richard J. Oldenski, M.D., and Elaine Ballou Yates for their helpful suggestions. John Lipscomb, former bishop to our diocese, found time in his hectic first year to read this work and write the following letter of recommendation. He believed in the need for this writing, and his support was a godsend blessing. Lastly, Jack Crothers will always remain my very favorite wordsmith.

A Message from John B. Lipscomb, Bishop of Southwest Florida

Dear Friend in Christ:

The life of prayer is the foundation of the life of faith. How we pray shapes our belief. You are about to embark on a pilgrimage as you explore the life of faith and the life of prayer in the words that our Savior, Christ, taught us to pray. In the pages that follow, you will be offered interesting facts that begin to open up the meaning of the Lord's Prayer in its own context. You are also invited to meditate on the meaning of this model prayer as it shapes your own life of faith.

The ministry of all baptized persons is supported by a thoughtful, prayerful, faithful life in Christ. This study is a call to a deeper walk with our Lord and Savior as you listen for His claim on your own life as a baptized member of His Body, the church. As you spend time with those life issues that confront us daily, you will be asked to reflect on questions that will guide you in your spiritual growth. There are no right or wrong answers. The reflections that you will do are opportunities for the Holy Spirit to speak within your spirit to call you into that deeper walk with Christ.

I commend this work to you. It is the fruit of the labor and pilgrimage of one member of Christ Body offered to each of us as a gift. I pray that God will use it and bless it for God's glory in your life. May God bless and keep you in your study of this prayer that is the foundation of our life of prayer and our response in faith to Christ, presented to us to call us into intimate union with God.

Yours in Christ,

The Right Reverend, John B. Lipscomb, Fourth Bishop of Southwest Florida

Introduction

People speak, write, and produce movies about the 'Gift of Life' but rarely, in a conventional way, do we hear anyone speak, much less write about, the 'Gift of the Soul'. Yet, no one can have one without the other. At the beginnings of humanity, our Creator bestowed the gift of a soul upon every human. Its primary purpose is to fulfil God's desire to establish a loving, respectful relationship with His creation. God's purpose is within the realm of possibility because, from soul to brain to heart runs the circular threads of longing. Within our humanness, we crave what our Creator craves. Spiritual steppingstones are the path that leads the way.

The four gospels relate our Lord's habit of not only daily prayer—but a life where everyday personal, intimate conversations between Jesus and Father flowed back and forth. Jesus heard, and lived by, God's Will. Throughout His life, our Lord followed the steppingstones our Father placed before Him. Prayer established that unbreakable bond. Even while enduring the agony of torture and dying on the Cross, Jesus did not subside from praying. His struggles in ministry and His painful, humiliating death is our proof that prayer strengthens.

Issues find answers, choices discover guidance, searching places us on the correct spiritual path. The Lord's Prayer is the most magnificent instrument in helping us learn the art of speaking into Trinity's hallowedness. Our Father, Jesus, and the Holy Spirit await our prayerful words. What better way is there than to begin with His prayer?

This writing offers volumes of knowledge about Jesus' Prayer. This reading will save you pouring through over one hundred and thirty books, articles, and other publications referenced in the bibliography listing. Internet sites will satisfy your curiosity about the background of this extraordinary offering that has changed billions of lives over twenty centuries.

The following pages do not contain historical information as you usually read it. There are no clear-cut beginnings or endings. There are no in-depth paragraphs of explanations on any given point. Instead, gathered here are bits and pieces of information that are unique and of interest. Its reading will place you on the road to genuine admiration and gratitude that we are the recipients of Jesus' Prayer. The packaging of this historical information is one that I hope will bring knowledge and pleasure to you, my reader.

This book's brief history serves a double purpose. First, this collection gives both flavor and feeling of the environmental background of our Lord. Second, this book helps explain why the Lord's Prayer is as meaningful today as it was when Jesus first made this offering.

What may become apparent from these pages is that humanity is unchanged. It appears that generations must face a forced variation of contradiction, strife, destruction, hate, slavery, and war to get to the other side. When a peer group reaches a stage in its growth, the positivity of opportunity in all the fields of love, freedom, and peace can finally occur. In the time of Jesus' ministry, people were seeking ways to have a better relationship with God and each other. This continual seeking sounds identical to the life and times of the peoples of the twenty-first century.

Life for this writer became blessed when I knocked on five doors and asked people to join my project of revising old teaching works into one small book on the Lord's Prayer. One entry was (figuratively speaking) my husband who once again offered his enthusiasm, patience, and interest in my writing. Here is what Jack Crothers has to say about this book, "No matter how many times I am reintroduced to its history, or listen to the insights of my wife, the Lord's Prayer continues to bring personal meaning into my life."

My upstairs neighbor, Marlene Brickmeier, "Reading this book's marvelously gripping chapters has definitely inspired me and made me so much more aware that prayer refreshes my soul and fastens the hook of belief. The fact that I had input to its pages fill me with joy."

A down-the-hall neighbor, Brigita Gahr of the University of South Florida, states, "What I find unique is how this author effectively transports the reader into the hearts and minds of key historical persons…these shared perspectives and descriptive scenes make history come alive."

Cheryl Renz, a downstairs neighbor, writes, "Several chapters made me sit up in wonder! I am a Christian but do not consider myself a very religious person, or a scholar, much less someone ever involved in a project like this one. Yet, I enjoyed working through the chapters, learning, and having input. BC's writing piques my interest to read more about the teachings of Jesus."

My third-floor neighbor Lee Jones writes, "We all need something beyond ourselves on which we can rely. My small participation in this Lord's Prayer project has renewed me, providing new insight into our purpose."

Their words have certainly touched my heart and reinforce a personal belief that no serious writer should ever begin work without first having a team of critics. They need to openly point out errors in sentence structure, unclear statements, unfinished thoughts, and the necessity for more information on a topic. My readers do this, and I love them! Without payment, busy in their own lives, each has willingly offered hours to share their insights, questions, and doubts throughout the writing. Together, they helped me be a better writer. Cheryl and Marlene had the 'eagle eyes' who, separately, found the smallest of errors in terms that changed literary meanings. Jack, my muse of a husband, continues to delight my brain with his intuitiveness in finding the exact word sought. Brigita strengthened areas of information by tying together points; and, bringing out greater clarity in sentence structure.

Lee is someone I cannot say enough about for he quickly became more than a reader. He took on the jobs of manuscript formatter, English instructor, all-around handler of multiple computer problems, and a meaningful listener when I needed to work through information inclusions or discuss theological issues.

Each of my readers has become more than a neighbor. Now they are personal friends. They have blessed both my life and writings. With a most exceptional pride and thanksgiving, I extend my heartfelt appreciation for their inputs on this book.

My book was written for them, for they are representative of the Christian Faith today. Members of the laity, their interest, support, thoughtful comments, and continual encouragement speak to the power and voice that feeds the strength of our Faith. We need to hear a lot more "*voice*" from laity from every corner of Christendom.

I pray you will enjoy the following reading. From these offerings, you will deepen awareness of the meanings behind Jesus's Prayer. You will gain a deeper understanding and appreciation for the prayer's historical significance. May these 'tidbits' bring you closer to the one we call our life's savior. I can think of no greater gift to offer.

In His Name,
BC

The Jewish Heritage of Jesus

Why did Jesus utter this prayer, then teach it to His Disciples and Apostles, and then on to the rest of the world?

Because it is a simple prayer with down-to-earth language; yet, so powerful, it continues—even after two thousand years—to profound the hearts of not only Christian believers but also the hearts of seeking people everywhere. Jesus offers this prayer because He knows that by using terms and phrases relating to and reflecting the never-ending 'human condition,' the Lord's Prayer will remain supreme throughout a person's prayer life.

His prayer begins with people's heritage, no matter where one is born or in what century. The 'Our Father' is of Earth, and what follows is of Heaven. Then back to Earth with human desires, hopes, fears, petitions, sorrow, protection, trust, and love. The prayer's Doxology (not original but an added liturgical and ecclesiastical conclusion) ends with the lasting hope found in all humans, that of needing a meaning to one's existence, the 'forever and forever' whether it be the family's lineage, a matter of historical significance, or in the soul's continuation in God's Kingdom. A large part of this ebb and flow stems from how Jesus and His heritage united.

Jesus's heritage is that of the Chosen People, the People of the Book (Torah), the 12 tribes of the Israelites, the Jewish citizens claiming their Promised Land, and the very first large group to whom our Creator made Self known. The rich heritage of five-thousand years of history, with all its marvelous tales, myths, and true-life retellings, taught Jesus that what God seeks is a person's open heart. Communicating the Lord's Prayer offers your heart to our Father because you can say the words with feeling, thought, remembrance, and planning.

This prayer is Jesus's crown teaching, for it clearly states His goal: Father and His creations are speaking with one another, sharing in life. There is nothing you must hide, run from, or keep secret. All is already known, yet still—with three heartbreaking words, *"I am sorry"*—all is forgiven, and forgotten! No wonder we pray this prayer from our hearts.

Notes of Interest on Judaism
and Christianity

Ellis Rivkin wrote in *Jesus's Jewishness* (page 226), that "...between mother and daughter religions, religions [are] bound by an umbilical cord which can never be severed." There exists an umbilical cord between the Jewish religion and all Christian churches. The mother is 'Early Judaism'; the daughter, 'Christianity.' As with many mothers and daughters, this has not been an easy relationship. Mother's Early Judaism had approximately a five-thousand-year history all to herself. These were informative centuries, a getting-to-know Creator Father in ways that enlightened, taught, benefited, satisfied, raised questions, and stimulated both fear and love.

From the beginning, nothing was easy for the 12 tribes of Israel. The relationship with their new deity, Yahweh, was challenging to comprehend, especially as the Israelites were just beginning their Faith's journey, struggling to understand what it would mean to be the chosen ones. Since freedom from a constant flow of conquerors was the goal, their motivation was high. At stake were cohesiveness, tribal identity, and eventual national respect. All they had to do was remain steadfast, listen to their prophets, and obey the signs leading the way. Sadly, it did not matter how many covenants existed between Yahweh and the chosen people. Repeatedly, these promises were broken. People were, and are, flawed.

The heritage of Jesus derives from these centuries-old, Jewish, historical events. One of the more meaningful ways of acknowledging religious heritage is to know and show appreciation for the arts and literature stemming from this inheritance. This, the 'Book People' did. The Hebrew Bible, our Old Testament, is a representation of that magnificent dowry. Introduction to our Faith's history is the Book of Genesis. Still, we are aware that the honor of being the oldest writing of the Old Testament belongs to the Book of Daniel, which dates from around 165 B.C.E. and is found between the biblical books of Ezekiel and Hosea. Daniel's book is a handwritten record of events surrounding God's relationship with His creation. It continues to be the first book to stress the philosophy (*noumenon*) of the Resurrection.

However, according to some Qumran Aramaic and Hebrew fragments discovered among the Dead Sea Scrolls, three Enoch books began its writings around 300 to 200 B.C.E., ending in 100 B.C.E. Until further discoveries, First Enoch is the oldest apocalyptic writing and is found in publications like *The Other Bible* and *The Old Testament Pseudepigrapha.*

In Book One, Enoch proclaims himself to be the seventh from Adam, and the great-grandfather of Noah. The books tell of giants, demons, and angels. It explains why some fell from heaven and offers an opinion as to why The Great Flood was a moral necessity. Interestingly, Enoch's writing tells of the reign of the Messiah. For this reason, biblical books Deuteronomy (OT) and the Epistle of Jude (NT) have brief citations of this work (for example, see Jude 1:14–15). Christian Church Fathers Clement of Alexandra, Irenaeus, and Tertullian referred to this work, but the later writings ceased to be canonical. Their reasoning might be because the Enoch books disclose a belief of the Messiah having a 1,000-year reign. However, the Ethiopian Orthodox Church regards the Enoch writings to be inspired scripture. Furthermore, its opening sentence in Book One is considered the very first sentence written in any human language.

This brief history is brought to you to demonstrate how the Hebrew Bible and the Christian Bible (Old Testament and New Testament) are closely intertwined. We share its writings because we share its history. Each book in the Hebrew Bible and ours tells something about God's characteristics and expectations. The books and letters, these 'testaments' explain the relationship God has desired to have with us.

They offer very graphic stories that show just how miserably humanity failed at achieving relationships with our Creator—and each other. Altogether, the Holy Bible is a remarkable book about failures, struggles, and hard-earned victories. It shows us what we are in the worst of conditions and who we can be in the best of circumstances. The entire work gives excellent 'how-to' examples for growth into fully functional, highly motivated, ethical, and Faithful steadfast human beings. The created Garden of Eden (our beautiful Earth) is a place for us to live happily, safely, and lovingly.

The phrase 'Old Testament' is always written under duress by your author, for the title is a definite misnomer. The Jewish religion does not acknowledge the terms 'Old' or 'Testament', for neither is historically sound. It is a fact that the ancient Christian hierarchy appropriated these four Jewish writings: the Torah (first five books of the Bible), the Major Prophets, the Minor Prophets, and the Writings. The church fathers (theologians and doctrinal writers during the foundation of the Latin and Greek Churches), without asking permission of their Hebrew brethren, 'acquired' these groups of writings and made them into the Christian's Holy Bible 'Old Testament'. Perhaps this was a way for the church fathers to recognize our Faith's roots. It is also a tie-in with the time before, providing both a background and a history. Christians today readily acknowledge Jesus's Jewish heritage. We are thankful to have a record of the beginnings of our religious beliefs. But still, a *"Do you mind?"* would have been nice.

As a final word concerning the Hebrew literature heritage, consider how our Old Testament consists of the Jewish Torah, Major Prophets, Minor Prophets, and the Writings. In Hebrew, the TANACH is a collection of Jewish writings broken down in this manner:

T   = Torah (the Pentateuch or Five Books of Moses)
N   = Nebiim (Prophets)
CH   = Chetubim (Writings)

TNCH = With its necessary added "a" vowel for pronunciation, the word 'TANACH' is formed.

TANACH comprise the Hebrew Bible.

- The various books which form the Jewish Bible or Hebrew Scriptures (Biblia Hebraica) began forming its literary shape sometime between the tenth and ninth century B.C.E.
- The name 'Bible' derives from the Greek word 'Biblia' meaning 'small books'.
- According to Jonathan Petersen of Bible Gateway, the Letter of James was the first New Testament written between 44 to 49 C.E., with Galatians following, 49 to 50 C.E.

The Gospels of Mark and Matthew appeared between 50 and 60 C.E., and the Gospel of Luke between 60 to 61 C.E., and the Gospel of John between 80 to 90 C.E. It was 11–16 years after Jesus's death for James's letter to appear. And a span of 17–27 years after the death of our Lord in 33 C.E. for the first gospel to be written. Thanks to the devout men who put their knowledge and longings to pen, we have writings that help us understand the life and times of our Lord and the creation of the Christian Faith.

Excluding John's Gospel and Acts of the Apostles, the New Testament (apart from a few remarks) stands as an example of the peaceful coexistence between Jew and Gentile. We find that in the Synoptic (similar theme) Gospels of Matthew, Mark, and Luke, the words *Ioudaios* (Jew) or *Ioudaioi* (Jews) appear sixteen times, mostly in the passion narratives. Again, excluding John or Acts, the two words appear less than thirty times in the rest of the Christian Testament. For most of these thirty times, the title 'Jew' or 'Jews' simply meant anyone who was not a believer in Jesus. Another example here of 'generic title use' is the word 'Gentile'. It merely meant any person not of the Hebrew Faith.

Note that neither dislike nor any misguided 'hate' instantaneously occurred between the Jewish people and 'Christians' when Jesus suffered crucifixion upon the Cross. In the first place, mostly all followers of Jesus were of the Hebrew Faith. In the second place, the word 'Christian' (meaning 'follower of Christ') was coined decades after the death of our Lord (see Acts 11:26, written between 80 to 90 C.E.). According to historical events, and according to a study conducted by Cardinal Carlo Maria Martini, the term 'Jew' was not written by the church fathers in any pejorative sense until the fifth century.

Looking at it this way, it took five centuries of disagreements and dysfunctional behavior to turn mother/daughter into enemies. First-century Jewish believers preached that their Messiah had lived among them, teaching the way to a New Life. Rabbi Jesus sermonized a Truth in a manner they had not heard before. It was no longer necessary to adhere to the 613 religious laws that stifled one's ability to question mostly manmade commandments arriving from the Temple Sanhedrin priests, the Pharisee and Scribe sects, or the competing Rabbi Hillel and Rabbi Shammai progressive and conservative schools. To test Jesus, a Doctor of the Law asked, "Rabbi, which is the great commandment in the law?" (Matthew 22:34, NKJV Study Bible) Jesus answered that there are only two Laws: "Love God with all your heart, soul, and mind," as the first and great commandment. Second, "Love your neighbor as you love yourself." [This goes hand in hand with the Golden Rule, "Do unto others as you would have done unto you." Luke 6:31 and Mt 7:12.] Upon these two Jesus commandments hang all the Laws and the Prophets (Mt 22:37–40 and Mark 12:28–31). Just imagine how these two profound statements vibrated throughout the Jewish land! To offer an example of its societal impact, read in Luke 10:25–28 how Jesus's words are repeated back to him by a lawyer!

Consider what an average synagogue service must have been like after the death of Jesus. Imagine, for a moment, sitting on a plank against the synagogue wall and hearing one of the readings that relate to a statement that, in your mind, contradicts what you heard Jesus say. Another man jumps up and shouts, "*Wait. This is not what I heard the Messiah say. He told us…*" You can believe the rabbi is thinking that freedom of discussion among the untrained in the word of God is terrible for the Faith. He and other rabbis with the same thought were right to be fearful. Worship services did become contentious. Think of having yourself, your father, a son, or best friend miraculously healed by Jesus. Think of being in the presence of Jesus, hearing His teachings on salvation. Contemplate spending those days at His feet, hearing the Great Sermon, where He spoke on the importance of the gift of life. Jesus preached the need to live on a higher moral path in order to have healthy relationships with one another and with our Maker. Jesus lovingly told of how Father wants to be in our lives—and that the way to begin is to say our Lord's Prayer. It speaks of forgiveness and redemption, of love, of Faith, of self, and each other. His words changed lives. Sympathetically, this had to be a very difficult time for those who wished to remain faithful to their Jewishness,

Listeners of Jesus's messages orally transmitted them throughout Palestine. Jesus's prophetic ministry was the talk of the land, wherein every corner, His name and purpose created discussions, friendly, and definitely not so friendly. These discussions continued in their houses of worship. Persons sitting in the synagogue, listening to arguments between the rabbis and congregants, often found themselves converting to this New Life offered by the Jewish believers. Yet, more arguments grew into more division. The breaking point came when the Jewish Christians began to emphasize the Resurrection, naming Jesus as being the long-awaited Messiah. Recoiling in horror, the Jerusalem temple priests sent word to the sect leaders, and into the ears of the elders (community leaders), "*Stamp out this heretical talk.*" Of course, this was impossible.

At this stage, the distant drum of the coming change was dim but heard. Still, there were those who experienced the first of many shocks to come when the 'am ha'aretz (people of the land) refused, as a social class, to obey. The wealthy and middle class enjoyed their status quo, and they would fight mightily to maintain their status. To the elite, Jesus was an annoying prophet, a disruptive force to the stability of the highly structured religion, and a possible break in the carefully orchestrated stratified economic and social classes. The people, though, had experienced Jesus as their loving savior. Jesus walked their streets, ate their food, and drank with them. He healed their ills and lovingly taught what they understood to be the true meaning of life.

In the synagogues, unable to stop the conversations, the loud debates, the arguments, and, sometimes, the bloody noses, the painful decision for a schism became the only solution. Finally, rabbis and Temple priests told the Messiah believers to leave and find another place to worship. Imagine the heartbreak upon hearing these words. Five-thousand years of tradition, togetherness, growing, learning, living, and fighting common enemies—all gone. Who do you love more: family, children, community, your Jewishness, or your Jesus New Life beliefs? Or is the issue that you have heard others tell farfetched stories of unbelievable miracles, of a person who commanded the wind and the seas, made the leper's skin heal, and the blind achieve sight? See! These were stories, no more than tales for the spiritually hungry, the dissatisfied, and the lonely—words, tales—that are meaningless to the Hebrewites who belong, who love family and tradition, and who honor those who came before.

Despite these hardships and breaking with one's past, the numbers of Jewish believers grew. Yet, slowly, the picture of who were becoming Believers did change. Traveling Jewish merchants told their Gentile customers stories about Jesus. It became easier to find converts abroad as persecutions were beginning at home. Eventually, fierce persecution by Jewish religious authorities led Apostle Peter to preach in Jerusalem to Gentiles, while missionary Paul converted Gentiles in Phrygia, Galatia, Mysia, Troas, and Macedonia (Corinth). Ignoring warnings about Jewish animosities, Paul came to Jerusalem to evangelize. Apostle Peter died (by his request) hanging upside down on a cross, and Paul was martyred in Rome, though how and when is historically unknown. Our first two greatest evangelists: Peter, upon whom Jesus gave the responsibility of building His church, and Paul, who first struggled to find that balance between Jesus's Jewish heritage and the New Life message he was sermonizing to Gentiles—were both murdered. Fearful nonbelievers killed them, that same fear which continues to plague the Christian Faith today.

More persecutions followed in one terrible scene after another. In too short a period, a crisis erupted between Jewish synagogue worshippers and Christian (Hebrew) 'Brethren' church worshippers. Even the terminology of 'Jew' began to take on shades of a different attitude. In the single Gospel according to John, *loudaios* and *loudaioi* appear slightly over seventy times, and, in Acts, over eighty times. These numbers are significant, for they indicate the degree in changed meaning in the term. Regarding time and attitudes, it is interesting to note that the New Testament letters penned by Paul contrast Jewish Christians and Greeks, while the books of John and Acts differ Christians and Jews. Jesus would not have liked what had happened.

These changes in attitudes and temperaments did not occur overnight. For the Jewish people, the excessive brutality perpetuated by the Crusades was simply the beginnings of horrors. While there are always exceptions, pre-1880s European history writes how the Jewish people and Christians coexisted as neighbors, co-workers, and friends. Intermarriage was the one taboo, understood and appreciated by all; well, except for young lovers. Historically, attitudes changed. Anti-Jewish riots of organized destruction began to occur throughout eastern countries. In 1881, pogroms (a Russian word meaning violent mass attacks) began with Russia and Germany and eventually spread to all of Europe. Terrible atrocities continually happened to the people of the Hebrew Faith. It became easier to listen to outrageous propaganda rather than attempt to comprehend the loving and exacting relationship between the Jewish people and their God. The new reality established was that the two Faiths who shared one God separated. From this point on, there was no turning back. The break between the Hebrew and Christian religions were final.

Today, we are a people acknowledging the tragedy of these evils. An entirely different history between two peoples joined in a mother-daughter relationship might have been possible, but this possibility became squandered by the sin of past deeds. Heritage is a precious gift. The Old Testament is not viewed as our Christian history, but, rather, a piece of antiquity.

The Holy Bible's Old Testament begins with the history known as 'Ancient Judaism'. The stories of the patriarchs Abraham, Isaac, Jacob, and Moses, the songs of Psalms, and other writings cover a historical timespan of 1,500–2,000 years. Ancient or Early Judaism is pre-70 C.E. (before the destruction of the Temple of Jerusalem). Pre-70 is before a large portion of the Jewish traditions, prayers, and oracles were formalized and put into a manuscript format. After the death of Jesus, and with the spread of Christianity, Judaism changed.

The following diagram illustrates its evolution over time.

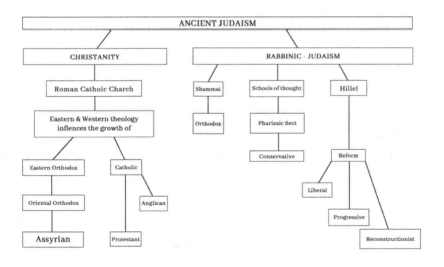

Judaism was primarily *Haggadah* (oral lore) and *Halakha* (oral law). After the Temple's destruction and the Roman War against the Jewish people had ended, it became a priority to gather, preserve, and record for all-time Jewish traditions, lifestyles, codes, and laws. Simplistically put, through this preservation process, Ancient Judaism became Rabbinic Judaism.

We forget that not long ago, the majority of the world's populace did not know how to read or write. People had to depend upon the oral traditions (the 'oral Torah' was based upon the traditions of the Elders) handed down within the familial groupings and religious institutions to understand their heritage.

Later, it was a privilege and a position of rank and honor to know the 'letters'. Knowledgeable persons wrote through their own biases and prejudices. These attitudes are one reason why the reading of historical events must include an open mind. In this manner, we can more readily accept new and more accurate information as it becomes available.

It has taken time for the daughter to mature and become a compassionate, understanding entity. For example, it took half a century for mother and daughter to climb over the ashes of despicable, inhuman holocausts to find understanding and forgiveness. Maybe this forgiveness was made possible by the countless heroics performed on both sides. Awareness of these deeds certainly helped in the maturation process—on both sides. It is an incomplete process, but, thankfully, parts of the faithful all around the world are coming together, sharing information, and acknowledging the rich Jewish heritage of Jesus.

As we continue to seek spiritual knowledge, let us remember to see the 'total picture.' The life of Jesus takes place in a period where Greek Hellenism and Roman conquerors ruled the world. Palestine is but an irritant, a place filled with religiously rigid people who have the audacity to worship only the One God while the rest of civilization worships countless gods. What a perfect time for the appearance of Jesus! Who else in the entire world had a religious structure like the Jewish people? A five-thousand-year old religion filled with an established theology, trained rabbis, worship services, prayers, rituals, laws, doctrines, edicts, and calendars for fasts, feasts, and agriculture. Tightly regulated were the impurity and purity laws, as well as the tithing and taxation laws. Into the picture walks Jesus. He turned the entire world upside down by speaking words of truth and religious freedom. Our Lord turned minds, hearts, and eyes toward our Creator of All, asking nothing for Himself. Jesus's goodness cost Him His life. Yet, He is with us still, and His teachings are alive. His offering of a New Life, leading to healthy living and salvation, guides our days. We of the Faith honor those who came before us and pray for those who come after us. Our rabbi-priest taught us how to pray, how to live, and how to die in peace and thanksgiving. Most importantly, Jesus offers us a home wherein Father, Son, and Holy Spirit are with us every step of the way.

Respectfully, let us pray we can make Rivkin's statement of "...between mother and daughter religions, religions bound by an umbilical cord which can never be severed," come true. We owe it to the Jewish heritage of our Lord.

Makings of First-Century Synagogues

The Book of Genesis relates how Yahweh initiated contact with Adam and Eve, His first human creations. The connection continued with His Chosen People's potential and bona fide leaders like King David, and with the prophets. Maybe even more importantly, anyone seeking to understand the troubled world in which they found themselves sought Yahweh's help. Yahweh always found them, no matter where they were or what they were doing, but where does one find Yahweh?

This is an issue that concerned Moses when he received word of his up-and-coming wilderness trek to the land of milk and honey. How would he and others contact The One Most Holy? What if there was an emergency? What if another plague broke out? What if the people got lost? Yahweh answered Moses's fears and questions in Exodus 25:2 and 29:46–47 by saying, *"Let them make me a sanctuary that I may dwell among them."* From then on, Creator Father would always be available to them. It would take Jesus to instruct the people on yet another way to reach out to Father for conversation, help, and guidance every day, not matter the circumstances, no matter what country they found themselves. But, first, at the beginning of a growing religion, reassurance was required, because people found security and comfort in structure, both in worship and in location.

The reassurance came via a 'tabernacle' which simply means a tent. According to Exodus and Numbers 9:1, the tabernacle took nine months to build. The tabernacle was carried each day by long poles. Toward dusk, before preparation of the evening meals, the Twelve Tribes gathered around the tabernacle, with sets of four named tribes gathering as a group, standing east, west, north, and south. According to Kevin J. Conner, in his book *The Tabernacle of Moses*, if one looked down upon the long tabernacle and the grouped tribes at its head and bottom, and the four grouped tribes standing on each side of the tabernacle, one could see the outline of the cross of Jesus.

Upon settling in Israel (1 Samuel 13:19), the tribes branched out, establishing settlements throughout the land. The biblical Book of Joshua, chapters 13–19, lends itself to descriptions of tribal land locations. The rise of villages, ruled by tribal leaders and elders, led to community worship until King Solomon built Jerusalem and the First Temple (Chapter 6).

The people returned to the Mosaic Covenant with the establishment of the First Temple, wherein Aaronic and Levitical tribes led the priesthood. Only in the Temple could the five sacrificial offerings be conducted: burnt offerings, the grain offering, the fellowship or peace offering, the sin offering, and the guilt offering. The Temple also controlled all aspects of the celebration of the three chief feasts, Passover, Feast of Weeks, and Tabernacles. Further Temple celebrations of feasts and fasts would be added to the Jewish calendar and placed under the control of the Temple.

Settlement across Palestine meant that not everyone could attend the Temple as often as required, surely not for daily prayers. This need became satisfied, as did the need to be close to Yahweh and have Him nearby, through the building of synagogues. The *Jewish Study Bible* states that "There are regular readings from the Torah, fixed readings from the Prophets, reading of the Five Scrolls on specific days, explication of Scriptures during or close to the public reading, including their translation into different languages, and extensive use of Scripture in the liturgy" (page 1930). Liturgically, offered were the recitation of psalms and additional scriptural excerpts from Song of the Sea, etc. This formula of a synagogue service continues to this day.

As part of the tradition, at the age of five, Jesus began to learn the Hebrew prayers, their terms, and their importance on how they guide Faith and daily living. Joseph started this teaching at home, and the learning continued in the Nazareth synagogue. By the early part of the first century, villages rarely had a synagogue, but most towns had one or more, while cities would have several worship establishments. The ideal was to have a worship building as a stand-alone, separate building. Funds raised for its construction came from donations or taxation.

Luke 7:1–5 recounts how the Capernaum centurion, a Gentile, built a synagogue for the people under his care. The noble centurion, highly interested in the Hebrew religion, did not become a proselyte, meaning an individual who formally studies the Faith to become a member. Instead, the populace knew the centurion as a 'God-fearer,' a Gentile sympathetic to the Jewish religion. Sadly, the gospels do not tell us if, after the miraculous healing of his servant, the centurion and his household became believers in Jesus and His future messiahship.

Villages and smaller townships would have had a worship area set aside in its community center. Community centers were a necessity, for it was here that populace concerns received attention. Usually held after prayer services, an elder ran the community meeting where everything was open for discussion with little kept secret. Talks revolved around the affairs of the heart, a petition for divorce, and a needed dowry for a poor bride. The date the tax on produce was due involved many owners and land leasers, as did how to resolve a longtime land-boundary dispute, for usually generations of neighbors were at odds. An unexpected arrival from a Temple Sanhedrin member wanting to discuss the widow fund always caused a stir, as very few agreed upon the who and its funding cost.

Also included was information on accidents, illnesses, crops, the poor, and the dying. The openness of these weekly meetings was an expression of the health of the community. In the open-sharing environment, cohesiveness and caring exhibited itself. When funds and talent for building became available, plans for building the much-needed synagogue proceeded.

Strangely enough, the exact origin of the synagogue (*synagog*) is unknown. Several possibilities present themselves within the literature about Israelites and Palestine. First, the roots might lay in the fact that community representatives gathered to pray when their rabbis attended sacrifices in the Jerusalem Temple. Another more traditional assertion is that upon the destruction of Solomon's Temple in 586 B.C.E., worshippers moved their services into private homes. From private homes would come either the building of a community center with its many public services, or the actual construction of a synagogue built in a style that met community needs. The oldest archaeological evidence of a synagogue structure is from the third century B.C.E., but hope continues for an earlier find.

Other historical evidence offers more possibilities:

- Tradition holds that the synagogue concept may have begun with Moses, as he relied upon the elders to instruct the people in the ways of prayer, worship, and obedience to the law; or,
- Synagogues may have originated in 621 B.C.E. during the Deuteronomic Reformation; or,
- The concept caught on when elders began meeting in the home of Ezekiel in the country of Babylon around 586 B.C.E.

The last possibility refers to the time of the Babylonian Exile from 597 to 538 B.C.E. Chaim Potok, in his comprehensive and highly engaging book, *Wanderings*, writes how, in 597 B.C.E., King Nebuchadnezzar II and his troops decimated the city of Jerusalem and destroyed the temple. Taken prisoner and deported to Babylon were the Judean's King, Jehoiachin, the city Jewish leaders, the wealthy upper class, and its artisans. The Temple's Highpriest and all other priests. Scribes and Doctors of Law were noticeably absent.

The Jewish exiles settled in existing Babylonian colonies, living life as members of the Hebrew religion manifested itself, as they still felt themselves members of the Jewish nation. It is a tribal fact that no matter where a Jewish group found themselves, their Faith and identity accompanied them. Daily life continued to include worship, prayers, and whatever rituals permissible. In Babylon, the religious structure came from the laity, as no ordained or hereditary rabbis resided in Babylon, not to mention that no synagogues existed. Yet, progress in the Faith made great strides. A great deal of credit is due to these laity leaders. It is through their leadership that the structure of future synagogue services established themselves. Around 575 B.C.E., the priestly source (P) wrote the books of Genesis through Numbers, and around 560 B.C.E., the Deuteronomist (D source) wrote the books of Joshua to Kings. The final section of 2 Kings was written in Babylon, as were the books of Jeremiah 39–42, 2 Chronicles, Lamentations, Daniel 1–6, Susanna, Tobit, Judith, the opening chapter of Ezra, Bel and the Dragon, 1 Esdras 3:1–5:6, and the final redaction of the Pentateuch. These are tremendously rich sources of the religion.

However, this was also a period of unknowingness. We have no way of knowing what rituals traveled with the captured into Babylon, or how the worship service unfolded during the Babylonian Exile. What rite established a pattern during the exile? With no rabbis for guidance, the elders led, keeping memories of prayers and worship practices that included observing the Sabbath, religious feasts and fast, and the practice of circumcision alive. *Encyclopedia Britannica* notes that this might be the period of synagogue construction. Archaeology has found no evidence that any synagogue existed in Babylon, meaning the worshippers probably met in private dwellings.

In 539 B.C.E., Cyrus the Persian conquered Babylon. He allowed freedom of religion and issued a decree that granted the exiled Hebrews permission to return to their homeland. The Jewish peoples' return was a piecemeal event, from 538 to 440 B.C.E. Considering that Babylon was the most magnificent city in the world, with its public buildings, palaces, Hanging Gardens, and temples, this was understandable. Why leave a place that had become home to return to a ruined city with no temple? Those who had returned to the homeland made constant appeals to those still back in Babylon. From time to time, the pleas bore fruit, accounting for the century-long piecemeal small group returns.

Returning exiles brought their worship practices back to the homeland. Over time, these combined with those already practiced by the Palestinian rabbis. As the returnees and rabbis worked together, a formalized worship service gradually developed. While the Babylonian exiles gifted the Faith with their writings and prayer developments, the temple gifted the priestly cult, offerings, and formalized sacrifices. A symbiosis developed wherein the Jerusalem Temple belonged to 'official' Judaism, while synagogues belonged to the people. R. A. Horsley's book, *Archaeology History & Society in Galilee*, contains a wealth of information on synagogues, some found in the following discussion. The symbiosis was a wholesome relationship as Temple and synagogues worked together and complemented one another's efforts. The Temple performed all the official, administrative, and political duties, including the all-important sacrifices, while rabbis and knowledgeable laity led local synagogues.

Mentioned earlier was that the building of synagogues is still a mystery as to the when and the where. However, we can better understand the transition from a community house to synagogue through the examination of terms. The term 'synagogue' is Greek in origin, meaning 'to bring together.' In this case, three Jewish functions were brought together under one roof.

- House of Assembly = *bet ha-keneset*
- House of Study = *bet ha-midrash*
- House of Prayer = *bet ha-tefilla*

Worship, study, and prayer services took place in the community centers before having a synagogue built. As the village population grew, towns developed, and with the increase in population, cities formed. First-century Palestine only had eight cities: Jerusalem, Sepphoris (called the 'metropolis of Galilee' after 70 C.E.), Caesarea Philippi, Tyre, Ptolemais (Acco), Caesarea, and Scythopolis (a Herod-built city in the Decapolis). Last, Tiberias, known as 'Middle Galilee,' stood between Upper and Lower Galilee.

First-century archaeology defines 'city' as possessing walls, gates, towers, chief rulers, and a synagogue as a fixed place of worship. A total of eight cities are mentioned. Joppa (today's Jaffa) was a 'city' though wall-less and gateless. It had a large population and Mediterranean Sea access that served as an international port and supply area for Jerusalem. Access to waterways, with easy access to the highway Way of the Sea (Via Maris), led to the growth of additional cities like Megiddo, Damascus, and Capernaum, names quite familiar in Christian literature. First-century historian, Josephus, speaks of Palestine possessing fewer than 240 townships. Eighty percent of the population was born and lived their entire lives in villages and hamlets.

According to Encyclopaedia Britannica, first-century international synagogues existed in Rome, Asia Minor, Greece, Babylonia, and Egypt.

Judaism, with its doctrines and traditions, rituals, rites, and prayers, fed the souls of a people born and bred to a specific religion through the daily offerings by the synagogues. They came in a variety of styles, known by different names, including House of God, place of worship, assembly, tabernacle, bethel, and House of Prayer.

Male Predominance

From the very beginning of the Jewish religion, male predominance established itself. 'Predominance' is a term that places males in the world of leadership, politics, and religion by way of his 'having ascendancy, power, authority, or influence over others' (*Webster's Encyclopedic Unabridged Dictionary*). The Jewish religion fell in line with what they knew, not necessarily of the male's worldwide authority, but from what they knew of their religious traditions.

By tradition, Yahweh created Adam first. Old Testament literature (written by men) has our Creator dealing almost exclusively with males, which, more than likely, was a show of adherence to societal norms. David was God's choice to be king. Moses was God's choice to lead the people to a land of freedom. Jewish oral tradition speaks to male dominance. Why would they think otherwise? The female species was an uneducated, second-class citizen, one step above a slave, and looked upon as property to be bought, sold, and ruled by family, religion, and society.

Justification for this action comes straight from the Torah and Christian Holy Bibles. Genesis, chapter three, tells the story of Eve bringing an apple to Adam. They eat and grow both wise and disobedient to their Creator who told them never to eat from the tree in the middle of the garden. Seeing their 'open eyes to the truth' (of their nakedness), God asked Eve, *"What is this that you have done?"* Eve replied, *"The serpent tricked me, and I ate."* Deflection and blaming another are two behaviors not finding favor in God's eyes.

The negativity against Eve, original mother to all offspring, is standing historically alone—and totally—responsible for the pains of childbirth, our desires for our husbands, and the fact that God ordained, "he (husband) shall rule over you" (Genesis 3:16b). This has always been a source of irritation to your author. Males have used biblical phrases (edited or otherwise) to keep women 'in their place,' subjugated, glass-ceilinged, and unequal. Now, to return to the matter at hand.

Religious law holds that whenever ten adult males gather (a *minyan*), whether in someone's home or an open field, a service could occur. Thirteen-year-old males took their rightful place in leading the worship service for, after his *bar mitzvah*, he became a full-fledged member, with all the rights of an adult male. Mistakenly, it is widely believed that the *bar mitzvah* formally began in thirteenth-century France. In fact, it originated from the seed of Genesis 21:8: 'And the child (Isaac) grew and was weaned, and Abraham made a great feast on the day that Isaac was weaned.' The Midrash carried this thought to its conclusion: 'The day that Isaac turned thirteen is the day when he was 'weaned' from his childish nature and assumed the responsibilities of an adult.' Jewish literature uses this verse as a source for the boy's *bar mitzvah* at the age of thirteen, where he would, thereafter, be accorded all the privileges (and responsibilities) of a man. Because the *bar mitzvah* ceremony has a scripture origin, its definition is 'son of the commandments.' A proud, circumcised, thirteen-year-old male participates in synagogue services and responsibilities.

Historically, the male super-eminent tradition would continue a flow of building and expanding. Second Samuel reads like a novel, telling stories of how King David captured Jerusalem from the Jebusites (a Canaanite tribe). Under his leadership, Jerusalem became the thriving capital city of Judaism, multiplying in population, as did the surrounding sparsely populated villages.

Males built communities, roadways, bridges, and piers along the waterways. Villages around the Sea of Galilee and the Mediterranean Sea, and travel routes like the Old Prophets route, the Way of the Sea, and the King's Way grew in population, becoming future townships and cities. Cities with large populations like Joppa, Caesarea, and Samaria (not including the Greco-Roman cities) would be among the first to build synagogues. Few villages ever had the means or talent to construct a synagogue.

At the beginning of the Jewish land development, due to the populace's low literacy rate, there was no prerequisite for worship buildings like a synagogue or study rooms. If no priest or elder was present, by tradition, only adult males with scripture knowledge could orally recite and lecture on the scriptures and lead the congregation in the prayers. It is still debated what the true number is be of village males who could read or write.

Why could only the males offer the service? Because a woman was unimportant, as they were property, without rights, without education, without leadership responsibility, seldom taught to read, rarely taught oral lore or law, and very infrequently considered filled with wisdom. First-century was a time when the concept of 'age' and 'wise' were identical in meaning. If a man lived into older age, life's experience automatically made him wise. Yes, this sounds like another historical misnomer—but maybe not when we consider that the life expectancy for males was twenty-nine years. Only four percent reached the age of fifty, and less than two percent reached the age of seventy.

Status of Wisdom

Considering the hardships of the era, one did grow up quickly. Wisdom in life decisions played an important role. Any male fortunate enough to attain forty-fifty years of age became an 'elder.'

Elders, and those filled with wisdom greatly influenced the worship structure. Elders not only led community meetings, but they also learned how to conduct a variety of worship services.

The following statements speak to the primary development of worship in the Jewish synagogues; that is, how 'Wisdom' and Faith were partners.

- A learned person was a highly respected individual. One could not be an acknowledged leader without the prerequisite of wisdom.
- Wisdom defined was a combination of knowledge, common sense, and study.
- This correlation between longevity and wisdom may be one of the reasons prophets were reputedly to be centuries old. This belief allowed prophets to have large followings and command such strict obedience from their people.

First-Century Education for Rabbis Seeking Diplomas

The formal education of rabbis grew in importance. Religious classes and instruction occurred in the community centers' rooms as well as in the synagogue buildings. Small educational centers sprang up, but two famous rabbinical institutes rose to the forefront, but not without controversy.

Shortly before Jesus began His teachings, two influential rabbis were fighting for dominance among the Pharisaic schools. Rabbi Shammai and Rabbi Hillel were literally struggling for the survival of their theological schools of scripture understanding and debate, Mosaic interruptions, and, most importantly for the future of their religion, the training of future rabbis wherein they earned a diploma.

Rabbi Shammai was a brilliant legalist, widely known to be an exacting and inflexible strict constructionist. With single sightedness, the rabbi saw the Jewish religion only in the sphere of 'Law'. All laws were encompassed, including the Law of Moses and all other laws with their codes. Rabbi Shammai was a tolerant and liberal constructionist whose mantra was: "Nothing is above the Law, and nothing is beyond the Law". There is nothing in life or about life that the law could not resolve.

Rabbi Hillel, on the other hand, devoted his life to humanistic teachings and is considered a great Talmudic sage. This man was brilliant in his understanding of human nature and man's innate need to please God by the fulfilment of his religious obligations. Jesus joins Rabbi Hillel in what was to become the Golden Rule (Mt 7:12), with Jesus stating, "Do as to others as you would have them do unto you." Sadly, Rabbi Hillel died within Jesus's lifetime.

A famous and much-retold account from the Talmud (*Shabbat* 31a) tells of a Gentile coming to both rabbi scholars and asking—in a blatant attempt of provoking them—to be taught the entire Torah while standing on one leg. Since any student of that time could state, the study of the Torah was and is a lifetime endeavor. Rabbi Shammai did become provoked and let no time go by before angrily smacking the man with a measuring rod. Rabbi Hillel, however, stepped in front of the man and calmly replied, "That which is hateful to you, do not do to your neighbor; that is the Torah, the rest is but commentary." However, in literature, there is a mostly neglected printed ending of "go and study it!"

Gamaliel the Elder assumed the difficult task of becoming Rabbi Hillel's successor. Toward the end of the first century C.E., Rabbi Gamaliel brought a formal structure to synagogue services. Additionally, he brought a variety of writings and prayers together, thereby establishing a congregational order to the worship service. However, it was not until the eighth to the tenth century C.E. that the Jewish religion had an authorized prayer book.

We come to a place in history where the synagogues' universal importance stands out. After the destruction of the Jerusalem Temple in 70 C.E., Judaism survived, in large part, because of the existence of individual and scattered synagogues. Prayer and study of the law and the prophets took the place of the Temple's sacrificial cult. This sacrificial system was a massive business, as each offering entailed animal's price, from a small dove to a whole bull. These funds, derived from religious taxes, provided upkeep for the care of priests, the temple, the widows and orphans, and other financial obligations. The sacrificial rituals provided a platform for the rites of burnt offerings, the offering of meal/cereal, offerings to heal feelings of guilt or the wrongdoing of trespass, the offering for peace, fellowship, and the severe, all-encompassing sin offering. The ritual of sacrifice would never return to the Jewish religion. Tying exile and sacrifice together is this ancient quote given to us by Dr. Ibim Alred in his book, *The Mystery Mission of Salvation in Christ Jesus*, "Forgiveness of sin is another way of saying 'return from exile'."

Synagogues made it possible for Jewish scholars, historians, priests, rabbis, and the ordinary people to come together to worship, study, and discuss. Synagogues kept people together, offering safety, identification, and a continuation.

Jesus and His Love of Synagogues

The Synoptic Gospels often speak of Jesus's love for the synagogues. His first childhood teachers, at age five, were the Nazareth's rabbis. His second childhood teachers were the Jerusalem rabbi-teachers when he was twelve years old. Through study, two impressions emerge. First, Jesus was an excellent student, taught well by His hometown rabbis. Second, Jesus found the Temple priests' wanting. Jesus answered every priestly question with wisdom. Jesus's answers caused the highly educated, trained rabbis to stand in awe of him.

For Jesus, there was much to dislike within the Temple's practices, especially the taxes levied against the people, which were overwhelming. These taxes included coins for tithing, sacrifices, widow's funds, and special donations. They also included a tax for reaching age thirteen for a male, and, for a female, age twelve; after that, becoming a yearly tax. Failure to pay meant one could not attend Temple service nor make a sacrifice. Taxes also included the choicest animal offspring born in spring and the choice of the finest first fruits.

In addition to the burden of religious taxes, the Romans were already heavily taxing the people. Travelers had to pay for the upkeep of roads and bridges, soldiers' support, and the care given to the wharves and piers. A toll was paid for driving wagons, riding donkeys, walking over bridges, for the soldier on duty, and the tax collector's wage. Wagon taxes were per axel. Types of food and amounts of goods taken to the market were taxed. Literally, people faced bankruptcy, starvation, the sale of their children, or the forced marriage of a daughter. Generational farmland went to taxes due to the owner's inability to pay.

Jesus also disliked the Temple's sacrificial practices. In John 2:13–25, we read how, during Passover, Jesus is furious over the shallowness of man and the rampant false beliefs in Jerusalem. In the Court of the

Gentiles, Jesus finds the Temple practices just as corrupt and polluted as in the past. Angered into a rage, he makes a whip and uses it to drive out animals and people. He overturns coin-filled tables. *"Stop making my Father's House a marketplace!"* This statement alone speaks volumes about the amount of pain felt over the desecration of what should have remained an eternal holy place, not only by our Lord, but also by the worshipers and prayerers who had to bypass the smells, noise, and disgust before entering the Chambers of Faith.

Jesus's experience with the synagogues was vastly different. He dearly loved the synagogues, the rabbis, and the worshipping people. In return, the rabbis respected Jesus, and, upon every visit He made to their area, they invited Him to read, deliver a sermon, and teach. The rabbis were thankful for Jesus because He healed their hurting people, both from physical and mental issues. The people loved Jesus, not only because He offered healings but also because He taught them. His storytelling, parables, and down-to-earth teachings offered to the *'am ha'aretz* what they received nowhere else. Sought after was Jesus's teachings on New Life, wherein experiences became meaningful, leading to the Eternal Kingdom. With popularity, these teachings took place while preaching in the synagogues He loved. There is no sign that Jesus ever attempted to change the synagogue practices. The Synoptic Gospels relate Jesus's embrace of the Sabbath and His eagerness to be present during worship service. What Jesus did do, which sometimes caused distress among the synagogue rabbis, was offer opinions on how laws and mosaic-renewed interruptions coming from the Temple hierarchy were stifling the Faith. There appear to have been rabbis who (in secret) agreed with Jesus.

Jesus had no abiding love for the Jerusalem Temple, its control over the Faith, its manmade teachings, its abuse of the people, or its political ties with the people's enemies. During a time of intense questioning, Jesus warned the Jerusalem priests of the Temple's destruction over three days. However, again, in another three days, a new Temple would be created (John 2:13–25). Was Jesus talking about building a new religion, or rebuilding the Jerusalem Temple, one created or recreated for the sole purpose of meeting the needs of the people, or was Jesus pointing to the Resurrection wherein He would be the new Temple? At the time of utterance, no one understood what Jesus was saying, not even the Apostles. Understanding of His prophetic words came only after the Ascension.

With the Temple's destruction, an untold number of rituals and rites disappeared forever. Gone was the office of the Highpriest and the hierarchy of the Sanhedrin. Other sects like the Herodians and the Sadducees also ceased to exist. The sacrificial system was gone forever. Jesus was the last sacrifice ever needed, as He died for the sins of all people. Jesus then lives on to reinforce His New Life teachings. The relics are no longer in existence. Today, the rabbi administration is more localized. The list of changes could go on. However, the one thing that has not changed is that the synagogue is still, and always will be, the place of worship for Jewish people worldwide.

Prayers During the Time of Jesus
Prayer Beginnings

Prayers have been a part of the human psyche since the beginnings of humanity. Over the eons of both great and small civilizations, rocks, mountains, the sun, the moon, and wooden or stone carvings were the recipients of heartfelt prayers. Once the Creator of All and humankind joined in a soul-inspiring relationship, prayer became a "service of the heart" as "You shall serve God with your whole heart" (Deuteronomy 11:13). Prayer is a Torah-based commandment, and prayerers also enjoy the knowledge that prayer is a precious privilege.

Two constants have been present in prayers, no matter what era or in what country: one of asking for help, and one of praise and thanksgiving for an answered prayer. However, asking for help has been the one more consistently heard in God's ear. Praise and thanksgiving are far too often an afterthought, or worse, not uttered at all. Prophet Isaiah was quick to point to the necessity of saying thank you in 12:4–5, "*And you will say in that day: 'Give thanks to the Lord, call upon his name, make known his deeds among the peoples, and proclaim that his name is exalted. Sing praises to the Lord, for he has done gloriously; let this be made known in all the earth'.*"

Prophet Isaiah was not the first one to offer the 'how-to' examples on prayer. The Old Testament gives one illustration after another of how and under what circumstances ordinary people, rulers, and the Jewish patriarchs and prophets prayed.

The very first biblical book, Genesis, begins with a story about humanity's ancestors, Adam, and Eve. Interestingly, there are sixteen versions about Adam and Eve's sin, repentance, children, lives, and death, all written from the 13th to 16th centuries, primarily in the

49

languages of Greek and Latin. The manuscripts of *Life of Adam and Eve* contains the first referenced prayers of repentance, as well as a death scene prayer from Eve who, before dying, "looked up to heaven, rose, beat her breast, and said, '*God of all, receive my spirit.*' And then she lay down and died" (*Apocalypse* 42.98).

Prayer began with the first history of humankind, and no doubt, humanity will end with prayer. The first recorded prayer in Genesis is not a prayer made by a Hebrew, but by Melchizedek, the priest of the Canaanite cult. In 14.18–20a, the priest blessed Abram in the name of his God, maker of the Heavens and Earth. Abram then gave the priest one-tenth of everything he owned, thus beginning the tradition of tithing (14.20b). Abram (now renamed Abraham by God) continued to pray throughout his life, especially for Sarah and the continuation of their family (i.e., nation). This founding nation's patriarch stayed in contact with God, most times with purposeful prayer, but also by merely, directly, talking things over with Yahweh.

The three patriarchs of Israel are: Abraham, followed by his son Isaac, and Isaac by his son Jacob. God renamed Jacob "Israel", the ancestor of the Israelites. Most oral traditions, lore, and recordings of their prayers can be found in the following Jewish works: *Assumptio Mosis—The Testaments of Abraham—The Testaments of the Ascension of Moses—Martyrdom of Isaiah—The Midrash—Halachah—The Babylonia Talmud—The Palestinian Talmud—Tosefta.*

One such memorable prayer lesson comes from Patriarch Isaac's wife, Rebekah, who left behind an insightful teaching. Rebekah, heavy with twins and tired of their battling and struggling within her, went to God in prayer. In Genesis 25:22 "she prayed, '*If it is to be this way, why do I live?*' And the Lord said to her, '*Two nations are in your womb, and two peoples born of you shall be divided; the one shall be stronger than the other, the elder shall serve the younger*'." (Verse 23) A metaphor of the twins explores the opposing forces of good and evil existing within each person. The story of the twins, Jacob, and Esau receives attention in the ongoing chapters of Genesis. Following the metaphor's plot, we see how evil wins out only when it becomes separated and isolated. The lesson here is that when we deny our dark inner side, we deceive ourselves and complicate the struggle. As difficult as it might be to accept our "shadow" side, we discover evil's purpose and find ways to make it serve good.

Prayer helps ease the journey of shadow exploration. This is one of the prayer's most essential functions and maybe why prayer holds a primary position in religious beginnings. Within everyone there is a drive, a need, or a desire to express, to seek. 'Seeking' is driven by one's Soul. Again, we refer to the Book of Genesis with an introduction to the birth of humankind. Referring to chapter 2, verse 7, Rabbi Jonathan wrote in the *Targum* a rabbinic understanding: "And the Lord God created man in two formations; and took dust from the place of the house of the sanctuary, and from the four winds of the world, and mixed from all the waters of the world, and created him red, black, and white; and breathed into his nostrils the inspiration of life, and there was in the body of Adam the inspiration of a speaking spirit, unto the illumination of the eyes and the hearing of the ears." Another interpretation from author Wendell Berry on this Genesis passage is that the dust did not embody a Soul, but it became a Soul—a whole creature. Definitely there are different interpretations to the term.

Biblical Hebrew's word for Soul is *néfesh*, meaning breath, inner being. The name translates into words of common usage. These include life, wind, person, people, inner spirit, spirits (angels, evil spirits), mind, heart, creature, and self.

The Greek New Testament refers to Soul as 'psyche', a close root cousin to the Hebrew *néfesh*. Does the Soul's craving for spiritual conversations, guidance, and answers stem from one's own mind, the subconscious? Or is the Soul more ethereal, its delicate thoughts searching the light in the heavens above? Is the Soul looking for rest or strength in its search for answers?

Cura, Latin for 'care of the Soul', calls for "attention, devotion, husbandry, adorning the body, healing, managing, being anxious for, and worshiping the gods." Thomas Moore's book, *Care for the Soul*, explains in detail the importance of recognizing the Soul's needs. In living any kind of life, multiple problems burden our Souls. Issues of anger, sadness, depression, chronic illness, loss of employment, divorce, death—the happenings in life cause the Soul to suffer blockage. Each unresolved issue hurts the growth of a person's spirit, and can ultimately change, or even halt, the traveled path of one's spiritual journey. We need to speak of our concerns in prayer, and prayer will respond back to us, uniting us with Father, with our Lord, with the Spirit.

Before leaving the topic of prayer beginnings, it is only right to address first-century women's issues and their prayer obligations. From the beginning, rabbis exempted women from more formal prayers, and the praying at set times, like the men were required to do. Exemptions were not a slight but a consideration due to the physical requirements of motherhood. Females married soon after their first menstrual, usually at the age of twelve. To us, in the 21st century, this sounds far too young, and an abusive cultural requirement. Yet, when considering the early age of death, and the awful high rate of infant mortality, this young motherhood was a practical necessity. Thus, rabbis excluded women from the *minyan* (the required quorum for prayer) as their unclean state of menstruation, their continued pregnancies, birthing, nursing, and their constant care of small children made praying at set times a physical and religious impossibility. However, women were required to pray once a day. They had considerable freedom in choosing what they wanted to pray, their only restrictions being that their prayer contained praise of (*brakhot*) God, and requests of (*bakashot*) God, and thanks to (*hodot*) God.

Importance of Prophets

Prophets whose prayers received attention include the Former Prophets of Jewish tradition. Their prayers are in the Books of Joshua, Judges, 1Samuel, 2Samuel, and first and second Kings. The Latter or Major Prophets are Isaiah, Jeremiah, and Ezekiel, each having their own testimonial books. The Christian scripture also recognizes Moses, Solomon, David, and Daniel as Old Testament prophets. A longer list of the Twelve or Minor Prophets includes Hosea, Joel, Amos, Obadiah, Jonah, Micah, Nahum, Habakkuk, Zephaniah, Haggai, Zechariah, and Malachi.

Malachi was the last prophet for four hundred years. The absence of the Holy Spirit speaking through the prophets brought silence to the Land. This grieved the populace as they were used to hearing warnings and corrections from Yahweh's messengers. The Hebrew people never ceased praying to listen to a prophet's word again, as this would be proof that the Holy Spirit had returned to their Land. The silence ended when Prophet Jesus began His ministry as His prophetic messages spread quickly, hungrily throughout Palestine.

What is important to remember is that the prophets' responsibility was not only in predicting future events. While this vital function changed the course of history numerous times with warnings and predictions to kings, a prophet's primary purpose was to call all people into obedience and to develop a trusting relationship with God. God's covenant with the people and historical circumstances shaped the prophetic messages.

Prophets spoke for Yahweh, carrying the message to those needing to hear the words of God. However, after the prophet announced the accusation, and then its judicial sentence, the description of the coming punishment most often sounded quite harsh to the ears of the rulers or the people. While they trembled in fear, the prophets prayed to God for mercy and for a change of heart. A prophet's request was usually granted because, once the prophetic words were uttered, the horrified people would immediately begin to pray, to repent, and perform almsgiving (*sedakah*). In God the Father's loving mercy, the dire Divine decree would be rescinded.

Prophets King David and Daniel significantly influenced the timing of prayers. The Book of Daniel consists of six stories and four dream-visions. Daniel (Danel) was a pious Jewish man whose work is considered apocalyptic writing, essential in Jewish literature as the work speaks of visions, the use of symbolism involving numbers and beasts, and has a developing angelology. This early Aramaic / Hebrew writing (during 536 BCE or shortly after that [the time of captivity in Babylon]) is also important to Christians as it also refers to the figure of the Son of Man, the Resurrection, and the End of Time.

- Relevant to both the Jewish and Christian beliefs is Daniel's reliance upon prayer. Daniel consistently offered private prayer three times daily as "he kneeled on his knees and prayed and offered thanks before his God just as he had done prior to this" (6:10).
- King David was a mighty prayerer who uttered this prayer in Psalm 55.18, "Evening, morning, and noontime, I speak and moan, and He hearkened my voice."
- Thus, it became mandatory to pray thrice daily. At these appointed times, a person abroad turned his face toward the Jerusalem Temple (after 70 CE, toward Israel). If present in the homeland, or a synagogue, he turned toward the direction of Jerusalem. If he was present in the Temple itself, he faced toward the Holy of Holies and offered his prayers in that direction.
- King David and Prophet Daniel may have been the originators of setting the times. The honor of having three prayers goes to

the Patriarchs Abraham for the morning prayer, Isaac, for the afternoon prayer, and Jacob for the evening prayer.

Prayer Elements

The Hebrew Bible's prayers contain abundant teaching lessons as they tell of pride, stubbornness, triumphs, failures, shame, desires, vengeance, and pitiful human natures. Jeremiah 14.7 speaks to how sins testify against us, while Daniel 9 refers to the sin of wickedness and rebellion. Penitence is a crucial part of Jewish prayer for the wrath of God turns to mercy upon showing Him a penitent heart. Prayers of intercession and repentance uttered with perseverance and humility change Father's heart, for Father *always* forgives when forgiveness is sought. Simply offer a true sorrowful spirit.

Biblical beseeching prayers are throughout the early books. From the men, Moses asked for help in leading the people. Hezekiah lost no time in telling God that He, the living God, had been insulted! Asa, King of Judah, prayed for help against the vast advancing army, which was prayed again by Jehoshaphat in 2 Chronicles 20. Ezra's Chapter 9 prayers were about evil deeds, great guilt, and shared sin. Isaiah prayed over his unclean lips.

Beseeching prayers from women have not changed since the beginning of time as they continue to pray for the welfare of their men and children. Prophetess Hannah prayed for the poor and the hungry.

As we read about beseeching prayers, we come to realize that some are misplaced or futile. God will not undo what has already happened, as a limb torn off will not be replaced, or a man praying for his wife not to be pregnant will not make it so.

Not all prayers are about asking for something or the fulfilment of needs. Prayers are needed to offer thanksgiving, praise, and consideration of God's requirements. Moses praised God for gifting him with strength and salvation. Worrying about where God lives, Solomon built God an ark so that He might rest and dwell among His people.

Jonah thanked God for being his salvation. Job prayed by singing praises to God. Solomon also offered two prominent elements of prayer, that of petition and thanksgiving. Combining needs with appreciation creates a coalition between the human and the Holy.

Through the Holy Bible's earlier readings, we learn from the devout, the troubled, the fearful, the ones seeking a specific outcome, and those not afraid to question the One Most Holy, or make a demand, or pray for the unusual, as shown in the following three examples:

- When told by God that his offspring will be as numerous as the stars (Genesis 15.8), Abram (Abraham) asked, "*O LORD God, how am I to know that I shall possess it?*" In other words, Abraham is asking, "*Is God's Word good?*"
- Hezekiah informs God of another's wrongdoing in 2Kings 19.16, "*Incline your ear, O LORD, and hear; open your eyes, O LORD, and see; hear the words of Sennacherib, which he has sent to mock the living God.*" (King Hezekiah)
- In case God has forgotten, reminding Him of a forgotten promise made. "*Remember the word that you commanded your servant Moses, 'If you are unfaithful, I will scatter you among the peoples; but if you return to me and keep my commandments and do them. I will gather them…Oh, LORD, let Your ear be attentive…*" encourages Nehemiah in 1.8–11.

As we read these prayers spoken by our ancient sages, we cannot help but recognize their similarity to our prayers. On bended knee, a sign or a direction is looked for from The One loving us. We eventually learn that every feeling and every thought—no matter how unwanted—is accepted as a show of our humanness and needs. Prayers relate a desperate desire to be cleansed by God. We need, once again, to be 'holy' in His sight.

All the different types of prayers feed our spirit. Prayer becomes an essential part of daily life. There is a fundamental need to remain connected, for we experience and thrive on prayer's high power. We live in trust, for we believe the promise, *"When he calls to Me,"* says God of the good human, *"I will answer."* (Psalms 91.15)

The Manner, Preparation, and Attitude in Prayer

Regarding prayer, 'manner' refers to a certain way a person approaches or treats the prayer offering. 'Preparation' speaks to the acts performed in advance. 'Attitude' brings in the complexity of feelings, thoughts, and a thinking process that combines the feelings and thoughts into relational (and realistic) speech. These general factors are present in these first-century prayers:

- In ancient times, it was customary (and still is) to pray aloud, not silently. When alone, or in the presence of others, a person prayed aloud.
- It was customary, and still is, to stand while praying, and for men to sway while praying. Swaying is not mandatory, nor is this approved by many Jewish men; yet it does remain a personal choice.
- One prays standing, in a reverent attitude, eyes down (though some say 'up'). Genuflections and prostrations took place at specific points in the recitation. The posture was straight, and one's voice enunciated softly and clearly.
- A mental attitude of thankfulness was essential as the very act of 'living' was precious. Free of illness, disease, or a wound was considered akin to a miracle. To experience love and respect among family and friends was considered a blessing. To resist temptation, to resist sin in any form, was looked upon as a gift of strength from God Almighty. In a land filled with death— from stillbirths to high infant mortality rates and death before age forty—getting through a day without hearing the news of

someone's death was a real cause for thanksgiving. Now, let us in the 21st century turn the above "was" to a definite "is" as Life is precious!

- 1 Samuel 12:23 quotes Samuel as praying, "Far be it from me that I should sin against the Lord by ceasing to pray for you." Samuel was the last of the land's judges and first of the great prophets. His words were carefully listened to, which accounts for their remembrance throughout the centuries.

- Clothing was prayer-appropriate, meaning modest (tzeniut), with a large prayer shawl (tallith or tallit) for those who could afford one. A typical prayer shawl was striped and fringed.

- A head covering was and still is mandatory when at prayer, when entering a synagogue or upon entering the first-century temple. Today, a kippa (skull cap) is worn, but wearing them did not begin until the eighteenth century. A Talmudic sage, Rabbi Nachmen, began to wear a kippa to remind himself that God was always above him. Both the rabbi's popularity and profound reasoning quickly turned the kippa into an appropriate prayer head covering.

- In Jesus's day, the 'am ha'artez wore a year-round, long piece of cloth around their neck, often reaching down to the end of the hem of their outer garment, the tunic. For the poor, this cloth would serve both as a blanket and a head covering when pulled over their heads for prayer.

- NOTE ON JESUS AND THE 'AM HA'ARTEZ: for all the negative writing about the 'ignorant' peasants, we do need to remember that Jesus was one, as He was not of royalty, wealthy, or considered middle class. Prophets are in a particular category, but, culturally, most came from the 'am ha'artez class—

- Note that in the first century, women wore cloth for head coverings all the time (though not when working in the fields); and, rabbis wore robes decorated with lines and fringes, with the ability to pull a hood over their heads.

- Included here is a sidebar on sacrifice and prayer. After the destruction of the Jerusalem Temple, the Jewish people could no longer offer sacrifices. According to scripture, prayer took its place as an appropriate substitute for the sacrifice of animals. This substitute was righteous, according to the words of King David in the Psalm 50:8–10: since God created all the animals of the world, why would He seek their destruction through sacrifice?

- Listen to what God had to say of animal sacrifice: "If I were hungry, I would not tell you, for the world and all that is in it is Mine. Do I eat the flesh of bulls, or drink the blood of goats? Offer to God a sacrifice of thanksgiving and pay your vows to the Most High." (Psalm 50:12–14)

- After the destruction of the Jerusalem Temple, the substitution of prayers for sacrifice took place at the same hours that animal sacrifice took place in the Temple, thrice daily, morning, afternoon, and evening.

What we learn from the Holy Hebrew Bible's readings is that prayer offerings were spontaneous, following no discernible rhyme or pattern. This began to change when daily prayers slowly became formalized, especially in the cities and in the Temple. The formalization of writing the prayers showed forth their rhymes and patterns. But prior to this, Hebrew prayers were not memorized; only their themes were repetitious, giving freedom for expression uttered around the theme. The prayerful words were unique and individualized. Prayers varied in length, from short to long, depending upon circumstances, and the individual's petitions. This is how Jesus prayed, leaving us His examples as found in the Gospels.

Part of the urge for prayer's spontaneity might be found in the Hebrew verb for prayer, *hitpallel*, with the root of *palal*, meaning 'to judge.' Hearing one's voice speak in prayer to God, either aloud or in secret, does open the mind to understanding feelings and a train of thought. In effect, a person can see flaws in action, feel embarrassed over behavior, suffer guilt from wrongdoing, and make commitments of change; thus, 'to judge' oneself.

Rabbis taught that prayer is a constant vital part of everyday life. It is not just an act to perform—nor is God to be called upon only when a need exists. For pleasure and thought and purpose, days begin with a prayer to God. The evening ends with a prayer of joy experienced, thoughts appreciated, and goals fulfilled. Thus, to God, a thanksgiving of life is offered. And during the high sun, prayer is made to God. In other words, God was, and is, never far from one's mind.

Kabbalah is a form of esoteric Jewish mysticism. Within its series of *kavanot* (directions of intent), its branch of *hassidism* emphasizes a depth of emotional and sincere connection to the actions and words of prayer. Therefore, while the prayers ahead are straightforward in print recital, be aware that the freedom to choose the time, subject matter, and emotional content still exists.

Prayer preparation beings with ablution—the washing of one's hands. Those following this practice in privacy realize that this is a wonderful set-aside time of preparation. Here is a luxury for meditation, the quieting of feelings and jumbled thoughts, for contemplating the petition(s), and the thanksgivings. The ritual of soap and water, watching the bubbles form, enlarge, disappear, and wash away, leaving behind only the cleanliness so appreciated by our Father (cleanliness *is* next to godliness). These steps create an atmosphere wherein one steps away from the world and enter the realm of joined communications with God. There is an incredibly unique term for this purposefulness—*kawwanah ha-kb*—meaning attention, intention, a concentration of mind, and devoutness of spirit.

However, we do know that time and space cannot always be of our choosing. Sometimes immediate help is needed, and we pray to God for quick decisions that may make the difference between life and death. God wants our prayers during this time. Beyond our panic, concern,

Father hears our prayer; as with the soldier, filthy from a foxhole, seeing death, and crying out.

We have the promise that he was indeed heard:

- "Though I walk in the midst of trouble, You preserve my life; You stretch out Your hand against the anger of my foes, with Your right hand You save me." (Psalm 138:7)
- "Fear not, for I have redeemed you; I have summoned you by name; you are Mine. When you pass through the waters, I will be with you; and when you pass through the rivers, they will not sweep over you. When you walk through the fire, you will not be burned; the flames will not set you ablaze." (Isaiah 43:1b–2)
- "I have told you these things, so that in Me you may have peace. In this world you will have trouble. But take heart! I have overcome the world." (John 16:33)

We are a people who need prayer answered. Cont. *"We have not heard back!" "Where is my answer?"* Here, a valuable lesson needs to be learned: perseverance in prayer is encouraged. We can never pray enough. Remember Moses. He continued to pray even after being told by God, *"Enough from you! Never speak to Me of this matter again!"* (Deuteronomy 3:26) Another example from Moses is where he prayed for 40 days, seeking intercession for Israel after the sin of his people's construction of the golden calf (Exodus 30). Our lesson is Never Give Up. When in spiritual direction with others and hearing a high level of frustration caused by unanswered prayer, your author always points out that our time is not God's time. Most often, as we later look back, we see where certain events, or other people's involvement, all had a part to play before God could answer our plea. We need to remember that God does not interfere with other people's Free Will—and neither should we! Thus, we must wait upon the LORD. Patience in waiting for a prayer's answer really *is* a virtue.

The Book of Psalms contains prayers ranging from joy to deep sorrow—and all the emotions in between. Psalms is sometimes called "the Hymnal of the Second Temple", for Hebrews have long utilized the songs and prayers of this written work in their daily prayers.

Jesus would have been familiar with the verses from this "Prayer Book of the Bible". This psalm book is extraordinarily helpful when a person is at a loss on how to express a feeling or touch on a painful subject.

First-Century Literacy Issues

During the first century, scribes penned prayers upon parchment scrolls, but not all rabbis could read, even though the ritual was to unroll the scroll and place it on the lectern. Literacy is what is at question here: an unknown shrouds' knowledge. There is no method we can use to lift the veil of times past. Out of necessity, we must depend upon archaeological findings, our ability to make mental connections as well as the utilization of insights into human nature. In renewing the much-discussed topic of the first-century literacy rate, two modern research tools examined Jewish writings and population estimates based upon whether antiquity named the area a hamlet, village, town, or city.

Percentage of Literacy in the Land of Israel (faculty.biu.ac.il) points to two Jewish books, the *Soferim* (11.2), and a Torah ruling in *t. Megila*, referring only to synagogues and townships, not to cities or villages (or, maybe the research means to call the 'township' a city). Not all towns possessed a synagogue building due to expense, knowledgeable builders, and available monies. The unearthed foundations of these buildings accommodated up to 50 worshippers. The article's relevant quote from the *Soferim* reads, "A town in which there is only one who reads; he stands up, reads (the Torah), and sits down, he stands up, reads, and sits down, even seven times." This statement means that only one person in town is capable of reading text.

The writings from the first century and their subsequent published books do not offer concrete details on populations and literacy. For this reason, Jewish writings like the *Soferim*, the *t. Megila*, and the *Midrash* are poured over and studied in exacting detail. In twenty-first-century literature, the following facts and figures are from Jewish historical works. Rural populations had a zero percent literacy, meaning not one individual possessed the ability to read. Six-year-old males went to school but not to learn reading and writing. Instead, all males learned about their ancestries and tribal history via oral tradition. The children's job was to memorize the family's history and pass it down to their children. (Females did not receive a formal education, though parents might have taught them limited amounts.) The rationale for this lack of training is that rural male children would end up spending their lives working in the fields. Why did they have to learn to read? What would even be available for them to read? Meanwhile, urban populations had a literacy rate of one to five percent, while the upper class of the urban population would have a two to fifteen percent literacy rate. Overall, the ability to read and write would probably be less than three percent in first-century Palestine.

This gloomy, highly publicized statistic continues to be challenged. Recently, Dan Falk (2016) wrote an interesting article, *More People Were Literate in Ancient Judah than We Knew* (*mentalfloss.com*), on a new study that begins with the issue of literacy back in 600 B.C.E. through a collection of inscriptions. The research shows how literacy was on the rise before the Babylonian conquest in 587 B.C.E.

To further stress the rise in literacy, the writing of the Midrash, a massive work of two sections, the *Halakah* (legal articles commenting only on the Torah), and the *Haggada* (consisting of narratives, homilies, and parables on the entire Hebrew Bible), was written, according to the resource *biblegateway.com*, between 1445 B.C.E. and 400 B.C.E. The Book of Job was the earliest book written, but its exact date is unknown. Nehemiah has a time of 424–400 B.C.E. Later Jewish scriptural writings, like Susanna, Psalm 151, the Maccabees four books, Wisdom, and 2Esdras, were written between 400 B.C.E. to 70 C.E. *Biblegateway.com* gives Genesis a period of 1445–1405 B.C.E. But your author falls back to the writing in *Encyclopedia Britannica*, which refers to the three strains or literary traditions found in Genesis. The Yahwist strain, speaking for Jehovah God, might have been written as early as 950 B.C.E. The Elohist strain, which addresses God as Elohim, was written between 900 to 700 B.C.E. in the northern kingdom of

Israel. The priestly strain speaks to the interest of cultic interests, and priestly regulations were writing around the fifth century B.C.E. Regardless of the lack of exact writing dates, we are looking at the growth of knowledgeable writers.

Falk's report on the literacy study continued with the examination of fragment writings, some found on pottery and others on parchment. Due to the difference in penmanship, names, and age of the physical findings, literacy might be higher than first believed. This study was written primarily for a computer algorithm whose input included information from "instructions for the movements of troops and the distribution of supplies, including wine, oil, and flour". Based on this research, the findings were that a higher literacy rate might be possible.

The research emphasized, "the political and military infrastructure that allows for the spread of writing literacy across different social classes". However, your author believes the algorithm should have included those who learned to read and write out of necessity. First-century archaeological recoveries include shopping lists from shop owners, food lists written by chefs of large estates, and ledgers conceived by accountants. Many research books discuss these lists. Also, think of the taxes collected during this era. The amounts due to Rome required the noting of minute details on goods, duties, and tolls. The numbers of taxes and tributes due to the Jerusalem Temple needed the collectors to possess writing and accounting knowledge. With these facts taken into consideration, we might yet see another increase in Palestine's literacy rate.

How did the illiterate get by without the ability to write or read? Professor Catherine Hezser points out in her excellent article found in *Academia, Jewish Literary and Languages in First-Century Roman Palestine*, that one's word was one's legal bond—if there was a witness on hand! Small landowners traditionally passed the holdings onto his oldest son. A first-century male could live his entire life without ever needing to write or recognize or understand a written term.

A scribe was hired whenever signatures for the signing of a personal will or deed was required. When an individual or tribal history was needed, their ability to recite long, oral stories saved the day. Oral traditions began with Moses and continued refinement until it became one of the highest forms of art and skill that any individual could possess. Excellent storytellers made great livings, being held in high regard. Elders in villages, towns, and even cities could recite the history of their place, the people, and their deeds. Not surprisingly, hours went by while listening to the storyteller recount exciting tales from the battles fought in the Maccabean wars, or stories of a forty-year life wandering in the desert during the Mosaic trek! Priests could recite hours of passages from their scrolls (which most could not read) and often conducted complete services through memory.

Daily First-Century Prayers

When reading this segment, please remember that the priests, educated elders, and laity who could not read, did conduct parts of the worship service through memory and probably quite flawlessly. Most of the following prayers were also said in the privacy of one's home, waking up, going to sleep, or with the family. Prayer began each morning and ended each evening. Prayers also took place throughout the day. The following prayers are what Jesus grew up with, and He prayed them each day of His life, but not quite. Remember, the following prayers in the rest of this chapter are the formal, written words that evolved and now, are part of printed literature.

Shema

An ancient 'reading' or 'proclamation' or 'recitation', which Jesus was familiar with, is called Shema, a Hebrew word for 'hear' (Hear, O Israel). Rabbis are careful not to call the Shema a 'prayer', for it is a proclamation of monotheistic religion. The public recitation of the Shema precedes prayers in the synagogues. The inclusion of additional prayers requires the Shema to be prayed three to more times daily.

The Shema began with Deuteronomy 6:4 but later expanded to include verses 5 through 9, which speaks to their requirement of total devotion to God. Deuteronomy 11:13–21 also became a part, with its emphasis on receiving wonderful blessings when obeying, "… loving the Lord your God and serving him with all your heart and with all your soul" (vv.13–15). However, there is a curse for the neglect of obedience found in verses 16–17.

This prayer is never said on its own or by itself, as it is not, in any real sense, a 'prayer'. Instead, it is more of a prelude to prayer, asking God to hear the following prayer(s). Shema is known as the 'Confession of Faith', stemming from three Pentateuchal (the first five books of the Old Testament) passages: Deuteronomy 6:4 and 11:13–21, and Numbers 15:37–41. The Shema is prayed in conjunction with Morning Prayer, Evening Prayer, the Benedictions, and other prayers.

Shema or *Sh'ma* rhymes with 'aha'. The term in biblical Hebrew means 'hearken', 'hear'. The very first sentence proclaims the Jewish Faith: "*Sh'ma Yisra'el, Adonai Eloheinu, Adonai Echad*". This first sentence or part (it has three) begins with: "Hear, O Israel: The Lord our God is one Lord; and you shall love the Lord your God with all your heart, and with all your soul, and with all your might." Jesus later added Leviticus 19:18: "Thou shalt love thy neighbor as thyself."

The original concluding part of the Shema reads, "And these words, which I command thee this day, shall be upon thy heart, and thou shalt teach them diligently until thy children, and thou shalt talk of them when thou sittest in thy house, and when thou walkest by the way, and when thou liest down, and when thou risest up. And thou shalt bind them for a sign upon thy hand, and thy shall be for frontlets between thine eyes. And thou shalt write them upon the doorposts of thy house and upon thy gates."

From the *Siddur for Messianic Jews*, the prayer book (pg. 35–36) offers this modernized version of the Shema, "Hear Israel, the Lord is our God, the Lord alone. Blessed be his glorious name whose kingdom is. And you shall love the Lord your God with all your heart and with all your life and with all your might. And these shall be words the which I command you this day on your heart and you shall teach them to your children, and speak of them when you sit in your house, and when you walk by the way and when you lie down, and when you rise up. You shall bind them as a sign on your hand and to be as frontlets between your eyes. And you shall write them on the doorpost of your house and on your gates. Hear O Israel, the Lord is our God, the Lord alone. Blessed be he whose glorious kingdom is eternal."

The Shema is also the last prayer spoken by the dying.

The lure of this recitation, its power, and its lovingly forceful proclamation of "The Lord our God, the Lord is One" will never fade in either Faith.

Morning Prayer

Morning Prayer, *shachar* or *shahar* meaning 'morning light' was, and is, the first words uttered upon awaking to the rising sun.

"Blessed be he who removes sleep from my eyes and slumber from my lids.

And may it please thee, Eternal One, my God, to guide my feet in thy law, and let me cling to thy law, and let me cling to thy commandments.

And bring me not into the hands of sin, or into the hands of transgression, or into the hands of temptation, or into the hands of dishonor; and humble my spirit, to submit to thee.

And keep me far from an evil man and from an evil companion; and let me cling to the good impulse and to a good companion in this world.

And grant me today and every day favor and grace and mercy in thine eyes and in the eyes of everyone who sees me; and bestow kindness upon me.

Blessed art thou, Eternal One, who bestowest kindness upon thy people Israel."

Because your author loves the following prayer, it has been added for your morning reading pleasure. Created by Rabbi Yannai in the third century, he taught his disciples to say an 11-stanza prayer with the rising of the morning sun, though I repeat only this:

"Blessed art thou, O LORD. May it be thy will, O LORD my God, to give me a good heart, a good nature, a good hope, a good eye, a good soul, a lowly soul, and a humble spirit; may Your name not be profaned among, or through us, and make us not a mockery in the mouth of men; may our end not be cut off, nor our hope be a vexation."

For those who have the time, a continuation of Morning Prayer is *pesukeid'zimrah* (verses of praise) which include Psalm 100, 145–150, a variety of biblical verses, ending with the Song at the Sea found in Exodus 14 to 15.

Afternoon Prayer

The afternoon prayers are called *minchah* or *mincha* and are named for the flour offering that accompanied sacrifice at the Jerusalem Temple. *Minchah* prayer time has always included a variety of prayers, such as *Ashrei*, a Torah reading (on Shabbat and public fast days), the Amidah, and the Tachanun (omitted on Shabbat, Yom Tov, and certain other festive days). The *tzidkatcha tzedek* is said only on Shabbat, and some prayerers include Psalm 84 and Numbers 28:1–8.

Evening Prayer

Evening prayer is known as *arvit*, 'of the evening' or *maariv*, 'bringing on night'.

The prayer is considered a facsimile of the Morning Prayer and is said before retiring for the evening:

"Blessed art thou, O Lord our God, King of the Universe,
who makest the hands of sleep to fall upon my eyes,
and slumber upon mine eyelids.

May it be thy will, O Lord my God, and God of my fathers,
to suffer me to lie down in peace and to let me rise again in peace.
Let not my thoughts trouble me, nor evil dreams, nor evil fancies,
But let my rest be perfect before thee.

O lighten mine eyes lest I sleep the sleep of death,
for it is thou who givest light to the apple of the eye.

Blessed art thou, O Lord, who givest light to the whole world in thy glory."

A modernized version of the Evening Prayer is:
He who lowers the bonds of sleep upon my eyes and
slumber upon my lids, and grants light to the eye:

May it please thee, Eternal One, my God,
to let me lie down in peace, and give me my share in your law.
And guide my foot to fulfil a commandment, and
guide my foot not to commit a transgression.
And bring me not into the hands of sin, or into the hands of transgression,
or into the hands of temptation, or into the hands of dishonor.

And may the good impulse rule over me, and may
the evil impulse not rule over me.
And protect me from an evil occurrence and from evil illnesses;
and may evil dreams and evil thoughts not disturb me.

And may my bed be pure before thee; and enlighten
my eyes, lest I sleep the sleep of death.

Blessed art thou, Eternal One,
who givest light to the whole world by thy glory.'

The 18 Benedictions of The Tefillah

Tefillah means 'the prayer', and benediction means 'blessing', thus the name of this prayer would read in English, *The Prayer of the 18*

Blessings. *Tefillah* and the 18 Benedictions are sometimes written apart, but both refer to the same prayer. Rabbis from the Great Synagogue (the Jerusalem Temple) composed the prayers. You will find the benedictions (blessings) also written as *Amidah*, *Shemoneh 'Esre*, or *Shemoneh 'Esreh*.

In Jewish liturgy, a benediction is any prayer that begins or ends with the phrase

"You are praised, O Lord" or
"Blessed art thou, O Lord."

Each segment is called a *beracha*, the Hebrew word for 'benediction'.

Plural segments are called *berachoth*.

Initially, there were 19 benedictions, but its name will never change from being called the 18 Benedictions. The title, 18 Benedictions, goes back to the end of the first century when Rabbi Gamaliel, while working at Jamnia, helped form the *Shemoneh 'Esreh*.

At the school in Jamnia, the Twelfth Benediction, also known as the *birkat ha-minim* or heretic benediction, was widely discussed. The blessing is a misnomer for the Twelfth is really a heretic curse. Two sources speak to the Twelfth. *The Babylonian Talmud* reads, "To blasphemers, however, may there be no hope, and may all who act wickedly instantly be destroyed; may they all soon be eradicated. Uproot the insolent, and smash, topple, and humiliate them soon in our time. Praised are you, Lord, who smash the enemy and humiliate the insolent."

However, the Palestinian reading states, "To blasphemers, however, may there be no hope, and may you soon abolish the wicked government in our time, and may [the *Nozrim* (Nazarenes) and] the minim [heretics] be instantly destroyed, removed from the Book of Life, and not written up with the righteous. Praised are you, Lord, who humiliates the insolent."

'*Nozrim*' or 'Nazarenes' refer to the Early Christians, the first Jewish Believers. The title points to the fact that Jesus was often called 'Jesus from Nazareth' or 'Jesus the Nazarene', earning His earlier Followers and Disciples the nickname of a member of the 'Nazarene' sect. A male's legal name stated the man's bloodline; as an example, Apostles James *ben* Zebedee and John *ben* Zebedee were sons of Zebedee. Calling their names in this manner means business is in the process of being conducted, or a stranger wished to speak to him, or a person knows him but not well enough to use the nickname. Both James and John were known as Boanerges (sons of thunder), due to their boisterous manners. Jesus referred to John as 'the Beloved', though this nickname is still somewhat in dispute.

We are facing how the Babylonian benediction prayer spoke in a generalized curse aimed at all heretics against the Faith. In contrast, the Palestinian benediction prayer addresses the problem of Jewish believers explicitly, citing the name of Messiah Jesus during worship services. Toward the end of the first century, this utterance was considered blasphemy. By this time, Christ-confessing Jewish people were seen and treated as heretics.

Following is a version of the 18 Benedictions that most scholars agree was used during the time of Jesus. Please remember they were not originally in these 18 numbered forms, but, rather, bits and pieces of the various benedictions were used both in private and liturgical prayers for centuries. Twenty-first century's *Shemoneh 'Esreh* is modernized in language, but we are attempting to discover those concepts in the prayers our Lord would have been most familiar.

In the following prayer, all verses that pertain to the rebuilding of the Temple were added after 70 C.E.

1. "Blessed art thou, O Lord, God of Abraham, God of Isaac, and God of Jacob, the most high God, Creator of heaven and hearth,

our Shield and the Shield of our fathers, Blessed art thou, O Lord, Shield of Abraham.

2. Thou art mighty and strong, and thou livest forever. Thou raisest the dead, sustainest the living, and givest life to the dead. Blessed art thou, O Lord, who givest life to the dead. (Note: In this Resurrection of the dead beracha, we find the influence of the ancient Pharisees.)

3. Holy art thou, and awesome is thy name, and there is no God besides thee. Blessed art thou, O Lord, the holy God.

4. Bestow upon us, our Father, knowledge from thee and discernment and understanding from thy law. Blessed art thou, O Lord, who bestowest knowledge.

5. Restore us, O Lord, to thee, that we may turn back. Renew our days as in times past. Blessed art thou, O Lord, who delightest in repentance.

6. Forgive us, our Father, for we have sinned against thee; blot out our transgressions from before thine eyes. Blessed art thou, O Lord, who forgivest much.

7. Look upon our affliction, and plead our cause, and redeem us for thy name's sake. Blessed art thou, O Lord, Redeemer of Israel.

8. Heal us, O Lord our God, from the pain of our hearts, and bring healing for our afflictions. Blessed art thou, who healest the sick of thy people Israel.

9. Bless this year unto us, O Lord our God, and fill the world with the treasures of thy goodness. Blessed art thou, O Lord, who blessest the years.

10. Sound the great horn for our freedom, and raise up a banner to gather our exiles. Blessed art thou, O Lord, who gatherest the dispersed of thy people Israel.

11. Restore our judges as in times past and our counsellors as at the beginning, and be King over us, thou alone. Blessed art thou, O Lord, who lovest justice.

12. For the rebellious may there be no hope, and the dominion of arrogance mayest thou quickly blot out. Blessed art thou, O Lord, who humblest the arrogant.

13. May thy mercy pour down upon the proselytes of righteousness, and give us a good reward with those who do thy will. Blessed art thou, O Lord, the trust of the righteous.

14. Have mercy, O Lord our God, on Jerusalem thy city, and Zion the habitation of thy glory, and on the kingdom of the house of David, the Anointed One of thy righteousness. Blessed art thou, O Lord, the God of David, who buildest Jerusalem.

15. Hear our prayer, O Lord our God, for thou art a gracious and merciful God. Blessed art thou, O Lord, who hearest prayer.

16. May it please the Lord our God to dwell in Zion, that thy servants may serve thee in Jerusalem. Blessed art thou, O Lord, that we may serve thee in fear.

17. We thank thee, O Lord our God, for every good thing and for the love which thou hast shown to us. Blessed art thou, O Lord, and to thee be thanks.

18. Grant thy peace to thy people Israel and bless all of us together. Blessed art thou, O Lord, who bringest peace."

What follows is a short, all-encompassing 18 Benedictions for those who were unable to complete the prayer in its entirety:

"Give us understanding, O Lord our God, to know thy ways;
to circumcise our hearts, to fear thee, and forgive us so that
we may be redeemed. Keep us far from sorrow. Satiate us on
the pastures of thy land, and gather our scattered ones from
the four corners of the earth. Let the righteous rejoice in the
rebuilding of thy city and in the establishment of thy Temple,
and in the flourishing of the horn of David, thy servant, and
in the clear-shining light of the son of Jesse, thine anointed.
Even before we call, do thou answer. Blessed art thou, O

Lord, who harkens unto prayer."

The Kaddish Prayer

The Kaddish is another type of prayer our Lord heard from childhood into adulthood. It is a prayer said for the dead. It is now both a liturgical and rabbinical prayer, but it was not used liturgically until after the fifth century. A leader reads the Kaddish, and the congregation responds with 'Amen'.

The rabbinical version begins with, "May His great name be praised and blessed…"

The liturgical text starts with, "May the great name of Him who created according to His will be praised and blessed."

Another form of beginning is, "Glorified and sanctified be His great name throughout the world which He has created according to His will."

All three prayers after that have approximately the same middle and ending parts as the following ancient form of the Kaddish:

"Magnified and sanctified be his great name in the world, which he created according to his will; and may he establish his Kingdom during your lifetime and in your days, and in the lifetime of all the House of Israel, quickly and soon. And say ye Amen."

Congregation response:

"May his great name be blessed forever and forever and ever. Exalted above all praises and songs, words of glory and consolation, which are spoken in the world. And say ye Amen."

In the 1975 Gates of Prayer, *The New Union Prayerbook*, the Kaddish continues to be a powerful prayer. The following excerpt is derived from page 622:

Before The Kaddish—

"Our thoughts turn to those who have departed this earth: our own loved ones, those whom our friends and neighbors have lost, the martyrs of our people whose graves are unmarked, and those of every race and nation whose lives have been a blessing to humanity. As we remember them, let us meditate on the meaning of love and loss, of life and death."

The prayer's preface continues with this powerful message,

"The origins of the Kaddish are mysterious; angels are said to have brought it down from heaven...

It possesses wonderful power. Truly, if there is any bond strong enough to chain heaven to earth, it is this prayer. It keeps the living together and forms a bridge to the mysterious realm of the dead. One might almost say that this prayer is the guardian of the people by whom alone it is uttered.

Because this prayer does not acknowledge death, because it permits the blossom, which has fallen from the tree of humankind, to flower and develop again in the human heart, therefore it possesses sanctifying power."

At the close of the daily common prayer, a personal petition is prayed, "O my God! Guard my tongue from evil and my lips from speaking guilt." Some call this a prayer against making slander, but maybe it can also be considered an injunction for God's help in keeping us from sin.

We end this section with reflection, a thought, and a prayer.

- Upon reflection, we discover threads of themes running through the Jewish daily prayers: hear, love, blessing/bless, kingdom, sin, evil, transgression, temptation, thy will, Father, awesome is thy name (hallowed), repentance, forgive.
- We see, and say, these themes in the Lord's Prayer.
- Now notice two themes not covered in the above prayers: forgiveness of others, and the righteousness of Heaven connecting to the acts on Earth (thy will be done on earth as is in heaven). Let us not be surprised that our Lord wants us to act upon the need to forgive others in order to enrich our lives, our soul's journey toward eternity.

- One attitude remains constant about prayer: it needs to be 'worship of the heart.'

In ending this section of daily prayers, allow your author to conclude with, "I do not cease to give thanks for you, remembering you [my readers] in my prayers. Amen."

Ephesians 1:16 (from the thoughts of Samuel in 1Samuel 12:23).

He Whom We Worship, Part 1

Heritage speaks of what one inherits, including DNA, birthright, legacy, endowment, and circumstances. Jesus's ancestry is that of a five-thousand-year Israelite history up to, and including, the era in which he lived. Heritage is the background image. Family is the foreground situation.

Our arrival into this world comes without choice. Blessed are those who are born into loving families. Fortunate are those who experience financial security as they grow into life. Gifted are those with memories of friends, laughter, celebrations, and a passion for learning and fulfilling dreams. Prayerfully, this auspiciousness continues unto death. Sadly, not many people—not even Jesus—gets to live an idyllic life.

Life's first years receive guidance from interactions with family members, religious affiliations, and limited exposure to the outside world. Knowing bits and pieces about Jesus's family, His love of his Jewish religion and its people, and His reaction to the political nature of Palestine offer us a snapshot into Jesus's thoughts. He brought together life experiences with that of His divine connection with The One Most Holy. These living seeds brought forth the power of the Lord's Prayer.

From Old to New – The Fulfilment Prophecies

This section is not a recap of biblical stories concerning the life of Christ. Instead, it is a collection of facts, questions, observations, and revelations about the life of the man called Messiah Jesus. He walked among us for thirty-three years with love and forgiveness in His heart and teaching in His mind. His connection to God our Father is unparalleled. Jesus's ability to heal, with a touch, a look, a healing thought from miles away, and His ability to command the wind and seas and inanimate objects cannot be rationally explained. We stand in awe and wonder. We also question. We want the truth about our Lord.

However, documents and archaeological findings have shown that some church historians made 'adjustments' when writing its history. There was a great need to 'prove'—especially in the beginning when prophetic predictions were perceived to be literal—that New Testament events correlated <u>exactly</u> to Old Testament prophecies. The following examples are a reminder to students of the Holy Bible that we all need an open mind when reading and studying 'historical' works.

Below are two excerpts from the book *Jesus's Jewishness*, edited by J. H. Charlesworth. The article is entitled, 'Jesus, Early Jewish Literature, and Archaeology.' The first excerpt is found in the tenth-century Arabic version of *Testimonium Flavianum*, while the second excerpt is from the Greek *Testimonium Flavianum*. The Arabic account offers a view of a man they believe might be making a historical difference to the world of religion, and they present facts as they knew them.

The Grecian account has a mission, as their rendering must convince readers that Jesus's birth, life, and ministry fulfils the Jewish prophecies in every instance. Underlined in this Greek translation are all words added by Christian scribes.

Arabic: "At this time, there was a wise man who was called Jesus. His conduct was good, and (he) was known to be virtuous. And people from among the Jews and the other nations became his disciples. Pilate condemned him to be crucified and to die. But those who had become his disciples did not abandon his discipleship. They reported that he had appeared to them three days after his crucifixion, and that he was alive; accordingly, he was perhaps the Messiah, concerning whom the prophets have recounted wonders."

Greek: "About this time, there was Jesus, a wise man, if, indeed, one ought to call him a man. For he was one who performed 'paradoxes,' surprising [probable meanings of Josephus], strange, or wonderful [Christian usage] works (and) a teacher of people who with pleasure received the unusual [truth]. He stirred up [win over to himself] both many Jews and many of the Greeks. He was the Christ ('so-called' or 'according to their opinion' may have been phrases used at one point). And (or 'but') when Pilate condemned him to the cross, since he was accused by the first-rate men among us, those who had been loving (him from) the first did not cease to cause trouble, <u>for he appeared to them on the third day, having life again, as the prophets of God had foretold these and countless other marvelous (wonderful or admirable) things about him</u>. And, until now, the tribe of Christians, so named from him, is not (yet?) extinct." (Ant 18:63–64)

From the genealogy recorded in Matthew's first chapter, we find Old Testament prophecies that were fulfilled: Jesus was from the line of Abraham in Genesis 12:3, Isaac in Genesis 26:4, Jacob in Genesis 28:14, Judah in Genesis 49:8–12, Jesse in Isaiah 11:1, and David in Isaiah 9:7.

Other details about our Lord's death fulfilled by Old Testament prophecy include:

- Zechariah 9:9, Matthew 21:4–10: the Messiah enters Jerusalem riding on a donkey's colt.
- Psalm 41:9, John 13:18: a friend betrays the Messiah.
- Zechariah 11:12, Matthew 26:14–16: the betrayal would be for 30 pieces of silver.
- Zechariah 11:13, Matthew 27:3–10: the money would be used to purchase the potter's field.
- Daniel 9:26, Isaiah 53:8, Matthew 27:50, 2Corinthians 5:21: the Messiah would die a sacrificial death for humankind.
- Isaiah 53:9, Matthew 27:57–60, Luke 23:33: the Messiah would die with criminals, but His burial would be with the wealthy.
- Psalm 22:1, 8, 18; Matthew 27:28–30, 35, 46; Mark 15:17–20, 24, 34; Luke 23:34b, 36, 46.
- John 19:24–25, 28, 30.

- Psalm 16:8–11, Isaiah 53:10, Matthew 28:6: the Messiah would rise from the dead.

We do not know if these testament events, Old and New, match without editing the verses. The problem with making just a single, provable, editing change means that everything else written—before and after—is also a suspect of having undergone an editing change.

Birth of The Messiah

Jesus was born during the reign of King Herod the Great, meaning that Jesus's birth date falls somewhere between 6 to 4 B.C.E., as King Herod died in the spring of 4 B.C.E.

According to the Gospels of Matthew and Luke, Jesus was born of virgin Miriam (Mary) in Bethlehem. However, in a time when places of birth were used as a means of identification, the New International Version [NIV] Gospels of Mark and John, and other books of the New Testament, refer four times to Jesus as 'the Nazarene.' Thus, the questions are:

- Were the Bethlehem birthplace statements made to fulfil ancient prophecies (see Micah 5:2–4)?
- Or was there no reason to reiterate the birthplace since it was well-known?
- Or, since the birthplace had already been noted in previous writings, was there no reason to reiterate it?
- Or were the Gentile Gospel authors not familiar with the messianic prophecy?

A point to be made is that Jesus could have been born at Bethlehem and still be known as a 'Nazarene.' Few people would have known about His birth, since, soon afterward, His family fled to Egypt to escape the wrath of King Herod. Hearing of a child born to be king, he sent in soldiers to slaughter all male newborns. Upon the family's return, while Jesus was a young boy, the family settled in Nazareth, becoming the 'hometown' of Jesus.

The ancient prophecies foretold that the Messiah would be of the Davidic bloodline, referred to as a 'sonship.' Steps were taken in the first chapter of Matthew's Gospel, as well as the third chapter of Luke's Gospel, to prove such a kinship. Unfortunately, it is a futile tracing, for Davidic descent originates through the familial males. In this case, Joseph. If you define 'virgin' as one who has not 'known' a male, then the logical conclusion is that Jesus is not the prophetic Messiah of Davidic lineage. This lineage would come from Mary's side of the family, and when Mary received the title of 'perpetual virgin,' Jesus's birth would logically no longer be a part of the Davidic bloodline.

However, a matter usually not discussed is Jesus's adoption by Joseph and, through this espousal, Jesus was given all the rights and privileges that Joseph legally and religiously enjoyed. These privileges were prestigious and considerable since Joseph was of David's lineage. This adoption, according to Jewish Law, occurred when Joseph presented Jesus at the Temple on the eighth day after birth, so that Jesus could be circumcised (Luke 2:21–27). Today, adoptions involve lawyers and legal papers with multiple signatures. Not so in the first century where, by Law, only a father could bring his son to the temple to be circumcised. A public presentation with a temple circumcision, a 'father' thus presents his son.

Another way to understand the virgin birth is to look at definitions stemming from that time. Virgin, *batulah*, is defined as a young female who has reached puberty, usually at the age of twelve years. Due to her young age, she is considered sexually pure, in a virginal state, a girl-child. In Latin, 'virgin' means a 'maiden,' equated to 'untried.'

Family Begins with 'Mother'

The family of Jesus consisted of at least nine persons. There were His mother, Mary; His adopted father, Joseph; four identified brothers: Jacob (later called James), Joses, Judas (later called Jude), and Simon; and several unnamed sisters (Mark 6:3).

Surmised from the reading of Luke 2:41–48, Joseph was alive when Jesus was 12 years old. Since there is no mentioned of Joseph in any of the Gospels after Jesus began His ministry, it is historically believed that he died sometime before the Cana water-into-wine miracle event.

In Hebrew, Jesus's mother's name is Miriam or Maryam, which means 'sea of bitterness' or 'sorrow.' Miriam and Maryam translate into Greek as Marima, which translates into the Latin 'Maria.' From Latin comes the English, 'Mary'. The first woman to be called Miriam is Moses's sister. According to Hebrew tradition, after that, all Miriams are named after her. It was a popular, and extraordinarily common, name of its period. In fact, so common that many named 'Mary' became known by the last name of the village, town, or city she was from, such as Mary Magdalene, to differentiate her from the other numerous Marys. Jesus's mother may have been born in Jerusalem of elderly parents or at Sepphoris in Galilee, as hypothesized in *The Apocalypse of Mary* and *The Apocalypse of the Virgin.*

According to the *HarperCollins Study Bible, NRSV*, the Gospel of Matthew circulated between 80–90 C.E., Mark in the late 60s C.E., and the Gospel of Luke between the early 60s to the latter part of the first century. Apostle John wrote his gospel either in the 80s C.E. in Ephesus, or while in exile on the Isle of Patmos, between 89–95 C.E. Marking Jesus's death at 33 C.E., we note that decades passed before pen took to parchment to further the ministry of our Lord.

Only the Gospels of Matthew and Luke carry the 'Christmas story,' Mark and John do not. Maybe the details of the birth story were too widely known. Perhaps the Gospel writers did not want to spend time on it or did not believe in how the story pieces fit together. It is doubtful that the Gospel writers did not know about the overly detailed tale. So, we will never understand why two out of four did not write about the birth story.

The Christmas story is one of the most persuasive examples of God's 'Will' and a pure human being. Presented to us is a young girl who is 'called by God' to have a child before having a husband and without 'knowing' a man. She accepted this call gladly, for she heard God's 'Will' and believed strongly enough to put on the line her Faith, reputation, and life (for, under Mosaic Law, unwed pregnant women were stoned to death). Mary left family and friends. She gave birth in the poorest of circumstances. To save herself and the child she bore, Mary fled to a foreign land. There, she resided with her husband and child for several years.

Old Testament prophecies concerning Jesus's birth and relationship with Father are in 2Samuel 7:12–15a, Isaiah 7:14, Isaiah 9:6–7, Isaiah 11:1–5, Psalm 2:7, 11–12, Psalm 72:9–10, Psalm 89:20–51, Proverbs 30:4, Micah 5:1–3. More Old Testament prophecy verses exist, but with just these examples, we can understand why having the connection between the Hebrew Bible and justification for the Christian era was so important to the Gospel writers. Messiahship branch references are in Isaiah 11:1, Jeremiah 23:5, 33:15, and Zechariah 3:6, 6:12. An important part of the prophecies involved the Messiah being from Nazareth. Nazareth's root word is *netzer*, meaning 'branch', and, religiously, branch is related to the Davidic root.

Mary watched her son grow, knowing He was not her son as much as He was God's. Jesus studied the Law and worked by Joseph's side as a carpenter. By age twelve, in His mind, Jesus had already left home, for His work was doing the Will of His Father. But, to Mary, He was still a child, her child. Both Mary and Joseph searched for Jesus in Jerusalem during the crowded Passover. When they finally found Him among the teachers in the Temple, Mary cried out, *"Son, why have you treated us so? Behold, your father and I have been looking for you anxiously."* Yet, Jesus wanted to know, *"How is it that you sought me? Did you not know that I must be in my Father's house?"* (Luke 2:41–49)

Knowing and letting go are two different things. When the time came for Jesus to leave Nazareth permanently to begin His ministry, Mary had to depend upon travelers to receive any word about her son. What she really heard, we can only surmise. Since we read pieces of Jesus's life in the Gospels, we can come close to guessing what Mary was told about her Son as Jesus traveled the countryside depending upon handouts for food. Jesus was homeless. Jesus slept nights in olive gardens. Jesus depended upon donations for clothing. He had just picked out fishermen to be Disciples and invited a socially outcasted tax collector to join this group. Not to be believed, Jesus even invited a Zealot to become a Disciple! Jesus was eating with sinners, Gentiles, and other outcasts. Jesus was chased out of town. Jesus had disappeared into the mountains. Jesus was curing the lame, the sightless, and touching the unclean, even lepers. Jesus caused a dead man and a dead child to rise! Jesus had a following. People were praising Him; people were cursing Him. Jesus was loved and worshipped. Jesus was feared and hated.

Influential people were out to get Him. Jesus rode into town, hailed as a hero. We can mentally set the scene as to what was told to Mary at the end: "I am sorry, Mary, but your son, Jesus, has been arrested." Finally, "I am sorry, Mary, but your son, Jesus, has been condemned to death by crucifixion, like a common criminal."

How many times did Mary cry out in anguish and pity for her son? Throughout Jesus's short life, how much worry, pain, disappointment, sleeplessness, and fear for her son did Mary experience? Yet, through it all, this woman of Faith continued to do the Will of our Father. Mary set us an example through her steadfastness. She was there for her son in the beginning as she was there for Him in the end. As Luke 5:51 writes, "Then he went down with them and came to Nazareth, and was obedient to them. His mother treated all these things in her heart."

There is another side to the above rendition, but not liked or thought about by many people. According to *Strong's Exhaustive Concordance of the Bible*, Jesus speaks the word 'mother' 30 times in the four Gospels. Only once does this reference refer to His mother, the other mentions are generic. Altogether, Jesus's mother, is mentioned by name a total of six times in Matthew's twenty-eight chapters, and these are at the beginning of his Gospel in the telling of the Christmas story. The Gospel of Luke also mentions Mary throughout the first and second chapters, again relating the birth and the flight to Egypt. Then, in Luke, like Matthew's version, Mary is not mentioned again, not even at the cross or the tomb, where the statement in Luke is a carbon copy of

Matthew: "Many women were also there, looking on from a distance...Among them were Mary Magdalene, and Mary, the mother of James and Joseph, and the mother of the sons of Zebedee," (Mt 27:55, 56; Luke 24:10). Biblical commentaries write that the mother of James and Joseph might be the Mary mentioned in 13:55, and again in 27:61 and 28:1, where she is called 'the other Mary'.

The Gospel of Mark mentions Jesus's mother by name only once in the sixth chapter. Jesus is preaching in His hometown's synagogue, and several townsmen are questioning, "Where did this man get all this? What is this wisdom that has been given to him? What deeds of power are being done by his hands? Is not this the carpenter, the son of Mary and brother of James and Joses and Judas and Simon, and are not his sisters here with us?" (verses 2b–3 NRSV)

For this discussion, the Gospel of John is an important resource, believed to have been written by Jesus's 'beloved Apostle,' John, during the time of his exile to the island of Patmos in the Aegean Sea. John was the only Apostle not martyred, living into his nineties. One thought is that his long life was John's reward for being the most faithful friend to our Lord. Still, another theory could be that John lived long enough to pen his account of the cosmic importance of Jesus's ministry, as well as the individual events in Jesus's ministry. Undoubtedly, John was the closest Apostle to Jesus, sharing in His concerns, offering encouragement, and defending His honor, words, and actions. As the beloved Apostle, John was a staunch ally of Jesus. John knew of Jesus's love for Lazarus, Martha, and Mary, and understood (though being jealous of) Jesus's spiritual relationship with Mary Magdalene. John certainly possessed knowledge of Jesus's emotions over the hostility shown to Him by His brothers, sharing these feelings as he writes about Jesus's unbelieving brothers in 7:19.

Indubitably, John would have known about the relationship between mother and Son. He knew about the relationship so well that he never mentioned Mary's name except at the very end of Jesus's life. This, in and of itself, tells us the truth about Jesus and His mother's relationship.

As further proof, John writes that, "Standing near the cross of Jesus were His mother Mary," (19:25). From the cross, with near death words, Jesus, "said to His mother, 'Woman, here is your son.' Then he said to the disciple (historically identified as John), 'Here is your mother.' And from that hour, the disciple took her into his own home," (19:26–27). This lack of mention of Mary's name throughout John's twenty-one chapters gives us a blatant clue to the actual relationship between mother and Son. Not even when dying did Jesus say, "Mary, my mother." Instead, He simply calls her 'woman'.

Two other biblical references offer clinchers to expressing the distant relationship between Mary and Jesus. First, shortly after Jesus appointed the twelve Apostles, people in his hometown turned against Him. "Then he (Jesus) went home (Nazareth); and the crowd came together again, so that they (the Apostles and Jesus) could not even eat. When his family heard it, they went out to restrain him, for people were saying, *'He has gone out of his mind'*." (Mark 3:20–21 NRSV) The *New Revised Standard Version* writes the two verses as, "And He came home, and the crowd gathered again, to such an extent that they could not even eat a meal. When His own people heard of this, they went out to take custody of Him; for they were saying, *'He has lost His senses'*." Though not stated in the various versions, 'family' most always meant all members. For Jesus, this meant mother and brothers.

A second incident occurred immediately following Jesus being accused of being crazy. Scribes (Teachers of Law) from Jerusalem said of Jesus, "He has Beelzebul…" (*Beelzebul* or *Beelzebud* was an ancient Philistine god, appropriated into the Canaanites god Baal. Later, the Abrahamic tribes turned it into a major demon.) Jesus then defends Himself by pointing out that a house divided against itself cannot stand. Though Jesus is referring to everyone's internal fight of fifty percent good versus the fifty percent terrible, we can also take His statement a step further, for He also refers to 'demons' that cause division in relationships, those outside of ourselves, especially that of family.

In first-century Palestine, family meant everything. Closest relationship, respect of bloodline, and one's family/tribal history, safety, emotional support, protection, the emotional and sometimes physical defense against tax collectors, or the Roman soldiers, or anyone who threatened 'family.' Throughout history, families, especially mothers, have been proud of the son who becomes a cleric. This was certainly true in Jesus's time. To have a family member become a rabbi was one thing, but to have a son known as 'prophet' rose the family's standing in their community and far beyond.

Yet, with Jesus's family, there were only three occasions when the New Testaments speak to them as a unit:

- Jesus's family was together in Cana early in Jesus's ministry (John 2:1–11). Relatives lived in Cana, and there was also a wedding to attend. When the wine ran out, Mary demanded that Jesus, "Do something." His mother was speaking! He obeyed, making wine out of water. His brothers were somewhere else in the crowd and missed Jesus's first miracle. At this point, some of Jesus's new Disciples were with Him, and they saw what happened. Mary observed, but no words of thanks or any other comment from her was recorded.
- Once, Mary and the brothers wanted to speak to Jesus, but He denied them by asking, "Who is my mother and who are my brothers?" (Mt. 12:47–49, Mark 3:31–35, L 8:19–21) Jesus answered His question by pointing to His Disciples and stating, "Here are my mother and my brothers! For whoever does the Will of my Father in Heaven is my brother and sister and mother." (Mt. 12:47–49)
- We need to go beyond the four Gospels to find a favorable statement concerning belief in the messiahship of Jesus by his entire family, but only after Jesus's Resurrection. Acts 1:13–14 describes how the Apostles, certain women, and Mary and His

brothers, James, and Jude, all prayed together in the Upper Room before Pentecost.

There are two traditional stories concerning Mary's later years. One is that she travelled with John to Ephesus. There, Mary remained until her death. The second story, equally supported by local tradition, is that Mary lived the remainder of her days in Jerusalem. Archaeological findings tend to support the latter tradition.

Jesus's Sisters and Brothers

SISTERS: According to Mt. 13:56, Jesus had at least two sisters, married, and living in Nazareth.

BROTHERS: Jacob/James, Joses/Joseph, Judas/Jude, and Simon or Simone (Mt. 13:55–56, Mark 6:3) are either brothers, half-brothers, stepbrothers, or cousins of Jesus. These were common names, as it was customary to name males after the sons of Jacob. Patriarch Jacob had twelve sons: Reuben, Simeon, Levi, Judah, Issachar, Zebulun, Joseph, Benjamin, Dan, Naphtali, Gad, and Asher. They married and, with their families, collectively became known as the 'tribes of Israel.'

Resolution on the actual relationship between Mary, Joseph, and their children are severely needed. For more than two millennium, this topic has been debated among popes, clerics, scholars, theologians, researchers, and religious writers. According to arguments put forth on this matter, the sons and daughters could have been (1) children of Joseph from an earlier marriage (Jesus's stepbrothers and sisters), or (2) his cousins, or (3) his actual younger blood brothers and sisters, making them His natural half-brothers and half-sisters.

The term 'cousin' comes from the fourth-century monk and biblical scholar, Church Father Jerome, who observed that, in the Greek language, 'brother,' 'sister,' and 'cousin' all have the same derivative. With further study, we find that biblical Hebrew (the Hebrew of antiquity) does not have a term for 'cousin.' From the fourth century on, Jerome's long-held tradition had Mary's sons as Jesus's 'cousins' prevailed, but recent re-evaluations speak to 'blood siblings.' However, until 'virgin birth' is defined to mean only 'young maiden,' total acceptance of Jesus having stepbrothers and sisters will still be a long time in coming.

What follows are arguments put forth on this question:

- Argument #1: Joseph was married before, and this previous marriage produced two daughters and four sons. Joseph was eighty years old when he married twelve or fourteen year-old Mary. Saint Epiphanius, a fourth-century Roman Catholic bishop, was first to espouse and then defend the doctrine of Mary's 'perpetual virginity.'

- Argument #2: The boys were actual cousins of Jesus, as they were the sons of Cleopas, who was either a brother or brother-in-law of Joseph.

- Argument #3: Like other historical disagreements, the etymology of language is often called into question. In reading Biblical Hebrew or Aramaic, Mark 6:3 may be defined as identifying Jesus as 'the son of Mary,' singular, 'the son' precluding any further children. Or the ancient writing could be translated as, 'a son of Mary,' meaning Jesus had natural siblings.

- Argument #4: Children were born to Joseph and Mary after the birth of Jesus. This argument comes from the statement in Matthew 1:25: "And he (Joseph) did not know her (Mary) until she gave birth to a Son; and he named him Jesus." In Old Testament vernacular, 'to know' a person meant one with whom you have had sexual relations. 'He did not know her until she gave birth' opens the door for the couple to begin a husband-wife relationship. If Mary married at the marriageable age of twelve, she was certainly young enough to birth six or more children.

o Added to this argument are two astute questions stemming from an article found in gotquestions.org in an article titled, *Did Jesus Have Brothers and Sisters*? First, why are Joseph's six children not mentioned in the story of Joseph and Mary's trip to Bethlehem to pay taxes? (Luke 2:4–7). Second, why were the six children not mentioned in the story of Joseph and Mary's exile trip to Egypt? They lived in Egypt for years, then returned.

- Another insight derives from a Wikipedia article, *Brothers of Jesus*, wherein the author reminds readers that when Jesus stayed behind in Jerusalem, conversing with the Temple priests, his parents left the group traveling back to Nazareth and rushed back to Jerusalem in a panic to find Jesus. It took three days to locate Jesus speaking with the rabbis. In Luke 2:41–51, no siblings are in this story.

- Your author finds one thing wrong with the argument that Jesus was the only child when visiting Jerusalem for the first time. If Mary and Joseph had six children after Jesus's birth, at least a couple of them would have had to be living by this time. One reasonable answer could be that no young children made this trip, as it is just too difficult—for them, their parents, and everyone else included in the group travel. A History of the Jewish People in the Time of Jesus Christ notes, "Everyone is bound to appear in the Temple at the chief feasts, except the deaf, idiots, children, eunuchs, mongrels, women, unemancipated slaves, the lame, blind, sick, infirm, and generally those who cannot walk." (Volume 2, page 51) Since walking was the primary means of travel, women back in Nazareth would care for the children. Note that women could be excluded, and this was due to their 'female' conditions.

- Argument #5: While dying on the cross, our Lord gave Mary over to Apostle John's care. Jewish religious law makes the eldest son responsible for the care of his aging parents. If he is dead, or incapable of performing this responsibility, the duty passes to the next oldest son. That Jesus chose not His 'brothers' but John, an outsider, proves that Mary had only one son and that the other six children were Joseph's from an early marriage.

- As an answer to this argument, no sibling would be around the crucifixion. Family members of criminals found guilty of treason or being enemies of the state (in this case, the Temple) would often be arrested.

o Fear of arrest is also a reason why most Apostles were not at the crucifixion. They feared for their lives, knowing that, more than likely, Temple soldiers were looking for them.

The lack of certainty in a familial relationship causes inconclusive writings when discussing the sisters and brothers of Jesus. This ambiguity is due to various interpretations and theological debates on the following factors: the 'virgin birth,' the question of who had the children, the 'perpetual' virgin state of Mary, and the Son of Man/Son of God interpretations. It appears that writers felt they were on shaky ground when any identification of the brothers and sisters was needed. Authors and scholars were uncomfortable in giving a definite relationship between Jesus and other family members, apart from Mother Mary who had (and has) some exceedingly strong defenders to the doctrine of 'perpetual virginity.'

These included:

- First to third-century Christian theologians Hippolytus, Eusebius, Epiphanius, and Church Father Origen believed that Joseph had children by a first wife who later died. They did not accept Mary having any children with her husband.
- Church Father Jerome, fourth century, referred to Mother Mary always, and only, as a virgin. His answer to the dilemma of scripturally named children between Mary and Joseph was that another woman named Mary was married to Clopas (Hebrew, or Cleopas, Greek), and this Mary and Cleopas had children who were known as Jesus's 'cousins.' Confusingly, John 19:25 states that Cleopas's wife, Mary, was the sister to Jesus's mother, Mary.
- Pope John Paul II pointed out that Jesus's words of, "Woman, behold your son!" refers to the fact that Mary's only son was hanging on the cross.

- Catholicism, the Assyrian Church, and the Eastern and Oriental Orthodox churches all believe in Mary's perpetual virginity.
- Martin Luther, John Wesley, Huldrych Zwingli, and John Calvin, all founders of their movements, were adherences to the perpetual virginity doctrine.

Both first-century Church Fathers Tertullian, and fourth-century Helvidius, known to be staunch defenders of seeking 'truth,' wrote against the doctrine of 'perpetual virginity.' Matthew 1:25 was the foundation of the argument, "He did not know her until she gave birth," opening the door for the couple of have begun a husband-wife relationship (argument #4 above).

Another support, though unspoken, occurred when the *Koine* Greek Septuagint Holy Bible was published. In the Greek language, 'brother' is *adelphos*, whose etymology is *a-delphys*, meaning 'of the same womb.' Another confusion occurred when the same work circulated (mostly verbally) among the early Christian community for 'brother,' and 'brothers' was an oft used term for all the male members among the fellows of Christ.

No matter what, Jesus and His brothers did not have a friendly relationship. The Gospels tell of the brothers rejecting, rebuking, criticizing (Mark 3:21), or ignoring Jesus (as they did throughout His three-year ministry)—behaviors which must have hurt our Lord tremendously. Younger siblings never expressed negativity against the parent(s) or older brother. This was the Jewish Law. Striking one's father brought on the sentence of being stoned to death. Criticism of a sibling could mean an explosion from the family for life.

At the time of the Festival of Booths in Jerusalem, Jesus's brothers urged Jesus to leave Galilee and go to Judea to prove His messiahship so that all Judean might see His works. They spoke these words—why? As a dare, or in spite, or to gain in popularity status, or out of hope because, at this point, they did not believe in Him (John 7:3–5)? Or was it merely because they wanted to see Jesus perform publicly His healing miracles? Bragging rights are so important! Jesus would not be healing at this time in Jerusalem because the authorities were looking for him. Better the brothers travel with Jesus to Judea and see His mighty works. John 7:8–10 mentions that Jesus declined.

BROTHER JACOB, (aka) JAMES: Biblical Hebrew '*ya'akob*,' Jacob, converts into 'James' in this manner: translated into Greek, '*Yaakob*' becomes '*lakdbos*.' Translated from Latin, '*iakobos*' becomes '*Jacomus*' from '*Jacobus*.' '*Jacomus*' then renders into the Old French 'James.'

Jacob was the oldest of the four brothers and was among the brothers when the crowd accused Jesus of having 'had lost his mind' (Mark 3:20–35). He was definitely not a believer in 'Jesus,, my brother the Messiah'. What happened that brought about his belief? What incident, or miracle, or Jesus-teaching, or talks with the Apostles reached Jacob's heart or mind? Unfortunately, we will never know the exact circumstances. Fortunately, Jacob did become a believer. His new name, with his new identification as a Hebrew Christian, was James.

It is Paul, not the Gospels, who stated that James followed Jesus sometimes during His three-year ministry. In First Corinthians 15:7, Paul noted that James became fully converted after a Resurrection appearance of his brother, where Jesus appeared to James even before the Apostles. James was among family members, praying before Pentecost, was present when the Holy Spirit descended upon the Disciples on the day of Pentecost, and was with the gathering of the Disciples after Jesus's Ascension.

Being present at these miraculous and world-shaking events changed everyone's lives. For James, he must have turned away from his old life for within three short years James was an essential and gifted leader in the Jerusalem church (Galatians 1:18–19). In 44 C.E., eleven years after the death of Jesus, King Herod Agrippa 1 beheaded Apostle James, son of Zebedee. Agrippa also attempted to have Apostle Peter killed, causing him, the church's first bishop, to flee (Acts 12:1–17, 15:13).

Jesus's brother, James, filled the void Peter's absence left. During those early years, James became known by two surnames, 'the Righteous' due to being a strict adherent to Jewish Law, and 'the Just' because of his conservatism and moderation in all situations. These attributes led him to become a popular, favorite leader among both the Jewish Christians and Gentile Christians in Jerusalem. Church Fathers Hegesippus (second century) and Clement of Alexandria (late second century) write that James became a bishop of the Jerusalem church, but there is no mention of this in the scripture.

Paul referred to James as one of the three 'Pillar Apostles,' meaning that John, Peter, and James held positions of importance in the upholding (pillars) of the Jerusalem church. The 40s were a difficult time for the growth of the Jerusalem church. It had to face the persecution in Jerusalem, the growing hostility of Rome, the horrendous theological and religiously ritual battles fought between the Jewish Temple hierarchy, the sects, and the *'am ha'aretz*, along with the constant contention between the Jewish and Gentile Christians.

As one holding a significant leadership role, James moderated controversial issues. One included the mission of Barnabas and Paul to the Gentiles, while, at the same time, affirming the mission of the pillar apostles to the Jewish community. As a sidebar, it is interesting to note that while Paul's credential is credited with being 'the evangelist/missionary' to the Gentiles, it was Apostle Peter who began the Gentile mission. Acts 10:1–33 tells a moving story on how Cornelius, a centurion of the Italian Cohort, received a vision wherein he talked with Peter. When Peter also received a vision telling him of the arrival of the centurion's servants, Peter began to understand that God also welcomed Gentiles to enter the Kingdom through Faith. This incident had a profound effect upon Peter, helping him realize his calling was different than Paul's and that both the divided but equal missions were serving God's purpose.

A second most critical issue discussed during the Council of Jerusalem (Acts 15:1–29) is when the near-explosive dialogues erupted over whether Christian Gentile males had to be circumcised. In the Hebrew Bible, circumcision between Yahweh and all Jewish males was considered a permanent covenant. Circumcision was a sensitive area, touching on Torah law. Emotions and tensions ran high, as the adult Gentile Christians believed the verdict would have them undergoing circumcision if they wished to remain in the fold, but James's mediation prevailed in a compromise. Out of this contentious meeting came the 'Apostolic Decree.' Gentiles were to abstain from, "The pollutions of idols and unchastity and from what is strangled, and from blood," (Acts 15:20). The letter from James was received with joy, as his words showed high tolerance and understanding. This letter was sent to the Gentile Christians in Antioch regarding their status in the church (Acts 15:13, 19; Gal. 2:1, 9–12).

It has only been recently that James was accepted as the author of the New Testament's The Letter of James. James, the brother of Jesus, was discarded as a potential author when choosing the New Testament books with a short history written about them. James, brother of John and son of Zebedee, and James, son of Alphaeus, were rivalled among scholars as favorites for its authorship. The doubt about James, brother of Jesus, was that the letter possesses an excellent use of Greek. Realistically, from its use of metaphors and idioms, it was suggested that, without any name ever mentioned, a Hellenistic Christian wrote the work before 90 C.E. The tradition now is that James did write the Epistle of James, for its strong moral content and Old Testament wisdom literature is in keeping with the knowledge of his period.

Sadly, James died by martyrdom, the same as all of Jesus's apostles, except for John. In his book, *James, The Brother of Jesus*, Robert Eisenman presents two stories on the manner of James's death. In the first story, James was executed by stoning by the Jewish Sanhedrin in 62 C.E. with the backing of the Temple's Highpriest, Ananus *ben* Ananus. The second story has James thrown from the Temple's pinnacle by some Teachers of the Law (Scribes) and Jerusalem Pharisees. The fall did not kill him; James was then stoned and clubbed to death by the group.

BROTHER JOSES, (aka) /JOSEPH: Joses could have been called Joset or Joseph. In Biblical Hebrew, Joses reads as Joshua and, in Greek, Jesus. Modern Holy Bible translations might read his name as Joshua (Luke 3:29). In Matthew 13:55, he is called Joseph. Joses's name appears four times in two Gospels:

- Matthew 13:55: "Is not this the carpenter's son? Is not his mother called Mary? And his brothers, James, and Joses, and Simon, and Judas?"
- Matthew 27:56: "Among which was Mary Magdalene, and Mary the mother of James and Joses, and the mother of Zebedee's children."
- Mark 6:3: "Is not this the carpenter, the son of Mary, the brother of James, and Joses, and of Juda, and Simon? And are not his sisters here with us? And they were offended at him."
- Mark 15:40, 47: "There were also women looking on afar off: among whom was Mary Magdalene, and Mary, the mother of James the less and of Joses, and Salome."

According to John 7:3–5, Joses, like his other brothers, did not believe in Jesus. In Nazareth, Joses was a part of the family delegation who went to retrieve Jesus and bring 'he who had lost his mind' home (Mark 3:20–35). Some writers feel that Joses never believed Jesus was the Messiah, but if we study terms like 'the family,' 'the brothers,' we do see Joses in the mix. Even though scripture speaks not on this, let us trust that Joses did, in the end, believe. With Mother Mary living in Jerusalem, it is reasonable to presume Joses and his family became Jewish-Christians and lived among the other believers in Jerusalem. Again, this is speculation, lacking credible resources.

BROTHERS JUDAS, (aka, JUDE): Jude followed in the footsteps of brothers James, Joses, and Simon. In the beginning, Jude did not believe Jesus was the Messiah. He was likely involved in the attempt to bring the 'different' brother—the one causing all the embarrassment to the family—home. However, after the Resurrection, Jude did become a believer. He and his family became followers in the Jewish-Christian group and probably moved to Jerusalem to be with other members of his family.

Jude, aka Judas, is mentioned in the New Testament only twice:

- Matthew 13:55, where the four brothers of Jesus are named.
- Acts 9:11a: "The Lord said to him, 'Get up and go to the street called Straight, and at the house of Judas (aka Jude) look for a man of Tarsus named Saul.'"

Jude accepted the fact that Jesus—as Son of God/Son of Man—was not his brother in the same manner as James was his brother. This difference accounts for the reason behind Jude's declaration of kinship to James and not Jesus the Christ found in the first sentence, the first verse of his epistle, The Letter of Jude, wherein he introduces himself as, 'Jude, a servant of Jesus Christ and brother of James.'

His was a letter meant to be more of a sermon, read aloud to all congregations. Jude was a Jewish Christian who had, by this time, established leadership credentials within the Christian community. His writing around 60–64 C.E. was forceful, which it had to be, for this was a time of 'false teachers,' of whom many were themselves sexually immoral, as noted in the Jude letter.

The New King James' Study Bible (2007) has a great first sentence in the introduction to Jude's letter: 'Few books in the New Testament have more to say to our generation than the Epistle of Jude.' Jude writes that the preachers' wicked teachings involved religious falsehoods, distortions, and self-serving actions that profit only themselves. Jude speaks to the danger of the Faith by noting the 'ungodly are not the heathen outside the church; they are the false teachers inside' (verse 12). Jude's listeners hear the hope offered: be mature in your Faith. Your strength will enable others not to be 'enticed or ensnared by error.' Good advice.

In an interesting sidebar, historian Eusebius reported that Emperor Domitian regarded the grandsons of Jude with suspicion because they belonged to the royal house of David. He had them arrested and interrogated. Upon discovering that the grandsons were but poor, ill-dressed Syrian peasants, the emperor dismissed them both, along with the charges of sedition.

BROTHER SIMON, (aka SIMONE): Simon is the least-mentioned brother of Jesus in New Testament literature, as little information is available concerning him. Simon's story is a carbon copy of Joses. He initially thought his brother mad; then, later, he believed in Jesus as the Messiah after the Resurrection. Simon is Jesus's youngest brother, put in order by the list of brothers' names given in Mt. 13:55–56, Mark 6:3. We do know that Simon was with the other family members in the Nazarene synagogue congregation when Jesus spoke there.

According to Mark 6:2–4, the family was impressed with His teachings but, at that time, did not believe Him to be the Messiah.

Simon probably fulfilled a role of small leadership duty in the newly, loosely organized Jewish-Christian community in Jerusalem, but no historical evidence offers this as proof.

He Whom We Worship, Part 2
Messiah Jesus

Who is this Jesus, a man so worshipped that, literally, millions of people have gone to their deaths to see that His teachings remain alive in the hearts of humankind? What words could be that important? How does this individual who lived more than 2,000 years ago still have the power to bring people to their knees as they utter His prayer?

Jesus was a carpenter, following in his adopted father's trade, just like the eldest son did in most every Palestinian Jewish household. Learning from one's father was an expected part of the trade traditions. Large towns and cities had more opportunity for young boys to join a trade's guild, becoming a master of the craft. Not so in Nazareth. Small towns and villages did not have guilds, as they were too underpopulated to support guilds in their functions of training, become assistants and increase demand for their skills.

Knowledge about the variety of woods, training on the art of taking accurate measurements without rulers, and the making of rounded wooden pegs all came from the patience of the father. Tools of the trade included pencils, a plane, compass, metal saws, adzes, chisels, ax, plumb line, bow drill, awls, squares, maul, iron nails, and files, as noted in the book, *Encyclopedia of Bible Life* among others. Mark 6:3, in the original Greek, states that Jesus was a '*tekton.*' Translated, *tekton* means carpenter, blacksmith, ironsmith, goldsmith, silversmith, or stonemason, builder of carts, or joiner.

Jesus, once having learned the carpentry trade from Joseph, would never have been considered an unskilled or semi-skilled manual workman. During that era, carpenters understood mathematics and were astute observationalists. As manual tradesmen, they were highly respected and admired for their knowledge, know-how, common sense, and abilities. They would be called upon to solve problems outside their specialty and were often villages or synagogue leaders.

As a *tekton*, Jesus had respect for skilled professions. Jesus did not, however, buy into the materialism of His society. We never read about Jesus buying land or seeking public office to glorify His name. As the eldest son and someone with Davidic ties, Jesus was certainly in a position to do so.

One thing Jesus did take advantage of was that of 'be-ing' a product of His time, for He lived, worked, talked, and developed His ministry according to the customs of His countrymen. Jesus believed in the Mosaic Laws and felt inspired by the twelve tribal and Israelite histories. He appreciated the spiritual and health value in His religious rites and rituals. Jesus understood the reasons behind the oral myths and why specific stories held prominence in the worship services. He would have felt pride in being Jewish, with its privileged position of being among the 'chosen.' Jesus's desire to communicate with The One Most Holy with the overriding need to follow the Will of our Father. The communication between them inspired Jesus to answer our Father's call with a determination that drove everything else in life to a lesser importance.

These overrides included family relationships and childhood friendships. His concentration upon His ministry was as pure as His heart. Jesus had a focused determination to bring first-century modernization into the stratified and stifling Temple's ancient way of presenting the Hebrew Faith. 613 laws regulating daily life was 612 laws too many for Jesus. Sharing Jesus's belief, Apostle Peter said, "We must obey God rather than any human authority." (Acts 5:29)

Our Lord had this commandment for living: "Love God with all your heart, mind, and soul." In Jesus's opinion, legalizing the number of steps an individual could take on the Sabbath, or whether it was legal to help an animal out of a ditch, was simply too much law. Those living under these laws felt their burdens and their suffocation. Centuries later, Saint

Augustine would set forth a reduction of Jesus's commandment: "Love God and do what you will." If God is loved—truly loved—wrongdoing will not occur.

Jesus spoke Hebrew, Aramaic, and Greek because they were the required languages for people in all trades and those in ministry. He lived a large portion of His life in Galilee and made yearly trips to Jerusalem. Both areas are known to have had Greek 'pockets,' where the growth and acceptance of Hellenism occurred. The changes brought into the Land by Hellenism began in the summer of 332 B.C.E. when Alexander the Great conquered Palestine. The spread of Greek culture, thinking, acting, and speech permeated the region. As a carpenter, Jesus worked for and worked among Greek-speaking people. It is reasonable that He had commercial transactions with Greeks living in Galilee, Judea, and the city of all trades, Jerusalem.

The importance of whether or not Jesus spoke Greek has to do with the way research is conducted on '*ipsissima verba Jesu*,' i.e., Jesus's own exact words. Some scholars think that if Jesus did know Greek, then more sayings could be attributed to Him and not to the work of the Primitive Church. For us today, to conduct a study in the Greek *lingua franca* is not difficult, for the language is still in use today. Even though it has gone through a modernization that all languages do, its derivatives are still traceable.

Scripture tells us that Jesus spent His childhood in Nazareth, which is still a pretty, small hill-town in the southern portion of Galilee. Lower Galilee is situated around the mostly serene Lake of Gennesaret (Sea of Galilee) and is an unchanging agricultural region. If these words conjure up a picture of a peaceful, uninteresting life, then the terms and images are faulty. In the time of Jesus, Galilee was an on-again, off-again hotbed of political and religious strife. It was not sedate. Galilee was near the highly used trade route crossing across the top of the Fertile Crescent, down across the Valley of Esdraelon, and on down into Egypt, first known as Way of the Sea, then – under Roman rule – renamed Via

Maris. Thus, child Jesus was exposed to peoples and languages from a variety of cultures.

As mentioned earlier, Galilee was religiously volatile due to the influence of the schools of Shammai and Hillel competing against one another for educational supremacy. Jesus, as a young Jewish boy, was exposed to all the elements of Palestinian pre-70 C.E. Judaism. His childhood would have been one of repeatedly hearing both sides of the debates. In first century C.E., the Shammaites had the upper hand, as their legalistic minds pitted against the humanitarian Hillelites. The battle was between logic and interruption versus cultural and societal lifestyle. It was also a war to win if the theologies embraced by either school wished to remain a religious influence.

Another consideration was the fractionally charged environment of Jesus's childhood. Politically, there were tremendous differences between North and South Galilee. According to the *Archaeology History and Society in Galilee* by Horsley, around 15,000 people existed in both north and south. But in many respects, it is like talking about two different countries. *Sketches of Jewish Social Life* by Edersheim notes that South Galileans were farmers and constituted the majority in the populace. Tradesman accounted for the stable middle class. South Galileans were proud, traditional, law-bidding, illiterate citizens who paid for scribes when they required a written statement and listened to the rabbis when they wanted to learn. Their families and the life they had made were prominent, not what was happening throughout the rest of the land.

North Galilee could not have been more different. The men were basically mountaineers, temperamental, independent, and fierce fighters who chose not to recognize those in authority. They battled with the Hasidim, King Herod, and the Roman Empire, ending in defeat with Jerusalem's destruction in 70 C.E. While in Rome, historian Jewish Josephus, with admiration, wrote about the North Galileans' battle successes while mocking the South Galileans whom the Romans called 'peasants' and 'stupid.' Peter experienced the embarrassment of having a guttural accent when questioned as to whether he knew Jesus. Mark 14:70 and Matthew 26:73 notes, "Surely you also are one of them, for your speech betrays you."

Regional people of different beliefs, philosophies, and nationalities shared the same small territory. Following is a list of the differing fractions to which Jesus encountered:

Qumran instructors and students + Teacher of Righteousness + Elders + Rabbinates + Pharisees + Romans + Sadducees + Samaritans + Zealots + Galileans + Herodians + Tetrarch Herod Antipas + Temple priests + disciples of John the Baptists + Essenes + local rabbis + Teachers of Law + Scribes + Highpriests + Hassidims + Rabbis Hillel and Shammai + Attitudinal differences among classes

Jesus was, in one respect, fortunate to experience the diversity of thoughts, attitudes, goals, and visions from these groups during His ministry. Jesus was less fortunate because He lived in a time when agreement meant immediate friendship, but disagreement could lead to death. Jesus's insight and knowledge allowed Him to debate with the best and most scholarly, for Jesus was a student of theology in its most profound level of the Faith. Yet, discussions occurred over the lack of opportunity to pursue higher education in the Nazarene synagogue. Repeatedly, Jesus proved that no one, not even the Temple priests, knew the Hebrew Scriptures as thoroughly as He did.

The Gospel of Luke points out, "And He came to Nazareth, where he had been brought up; and he went to the synagogue, as his custom was, on the Sabbath day," (4:16). Jesus not only attended the synagogue for service, as a child, he also went to a schoolroom located in the synagogue. All Jewish males received religious education from the synagogues' rabbi. In addition to the studies in the local synagogue, Jesus heard teachings when attending the Temple. Luke 2:41–51 relates how the parents of Jesus went to Jerusalem 'every year at the feast of the Passover.'

Along with hearing the lessons from learned rabbis, Jesus, then, would have been no stranger to certain aspects of urbanization: languages, political atmosphere, and religious rivalry.

But what happened after that? No local rabbi could have taught Jesus the accumulated knowledge He possessed. Except for the Hillelite and Shammaite schools, no other higher education opportunities were available, unless one wanted to travel into Greece or Rome. Based upon the sayings of Jesus, His profound and intimate knowledge of the *Halakha* (oral law) and *Haggadah* (oral lore), and the Tanakh (the Hebrew Bible), Jesus was an extremely learned individual, apparent in his speech, historical references, intimate knowledge of the Law, and the manner He presented information to His listeners. Jesus possessed the additional talent of being able to share this vast knowledge with the ordinary people at whatever level his audience required. So, where did Jesus acquire this knowledge?

Dozens of authors have alluded to a Qumran education, but, without evidence, no one wants to state it as a fact. Your author will. Without concreteness, the proof of availability speaks for itself. It takes no stretch of the imagination to visualize Joseph taking Jesus to the Qumran compound and turning Him over to the Teacher of Righteousness. Teacher then embraces Jesus with open arms, as he would have heard of this twelve year-old confounding the Temple priests and visiting rabbis with His intelligence and spiritual knowledge. Jesus would have returned to Nazareth during the summer months to help Joseph with his business. After a break of several months, we see Jesus returning to the Essene community to continue His studies. Jesus would, indeed, have thrived there. How happy He must have been among all those new learnings and feeling the respect emanating from His tutors.

His knowledge earned Jesus the title 'rabbi,' which means 'my teacher.' The men who were teachers of the Torah received this term of respect. 'Rabbis' were of two groups, those who lived and taught among the populace, and 'rabbis' who gathered disciples. As a unit, they traveled, teaching the word of their Faith. The number of following disciples informed the populace of the rabbis' knowledge of scripture heard throughout the year in their synagogue. For Jesus, rabbi-teacher enveloped the meanings of 'enlightened wisdom teacher,' 'teacher of heavenly truths/spiritual truths' or 'Kingdom bearer,' and 'itinerant rabbi.' Note that none of these titles derive from academic learnings; rather, they often touch on the divine gifts manifested from wisdom through the closeness with God, the Father.

Only later in first-century C.E.—after our Lord's death—did ordained rabbis with academic degrees appear. From that time forward, only degreed persons earned the right to be addressed as 'rabbi.' Thanks to the schools of Hillelite and Shammai, religious education for rabbis took on a structure. These studies, according to Moore's Judaism vol. 1, *The Mishnah*, included the teaching of tradition that included *The Midrash*, which is a higher exegesis of Scripture, with concentrated studies on both the law and the unwritten (oral) law. Also, the *Halakah*, the study of formulated rules; and, the *Haggadah*, the non-juristic scholarship of religious, moral, and historical teachings.

Jesus lived and died too soon to experience these intense decades-long studies, yet John 7:14–15 states that when Jesus went to the Temple to teach, "The Jews marveled at it, saying, 'How is it that this man has learning when he has never studied'?" Up until this time, in Jesus's ministry, most concentration was given to Jesus's miracles, even though He taught when crowds and enemies allowed Him to do so. In reading the first couple of chapters in John, we see how Jesus had to spend an inordinate amount of time in defense mode. In reply to *'How is it that his man has learning when he has never studied'?* Jesus gladly replied, *"My teaching is not mine but His who sent me. Anyone who resolves to do the will of God will know whether the teaching is from God or whether I am speaking on my own."* (7:16–17) It is difficult to be criticized when giving credit where credit is due!

Jesus had other titles besides 'rabbi.' To name just a few, Jesus was also called or known as: 'prophet,' 'the Galilean prophet,' 'the Galilean charismatic,' 'charisma,' 'miracle-worker,' 'the healer,' 'teacher,'

'Galilean rabbi,' the 'Hasid (a charismatic holy man) of Galilee,' 'the prophet Jesus from Nazareth in Galilee' (Matthew 21:11), a 'Hillelite,' a 'maverick Pharisee,' an 'Essene,' an 'eschatological prophet,' a 'magician,' a 'political rebel,' a 'political revolutionary,' and the 'reincarnation of Elijah.'

In addition to the above titles, Jesus was also called 'Son of Man' or 'Son of God.' This title, in part and very briefly, stems from two sources:

(1) The Book of Daniel, which is part of the 'wisdom' literature and one of the last apocalyptic materials (the disclosure [uncovering] of visions, dreams, and dreams allowing for 'revelations') found in both the Old and New Testaments. Daniel refers many times to the Messiah as the 'Son of Man' and identifies him as an angelic figure; and

(2) Psalm 110:1 states, "The Lord (God) says to my lord (Christ): 'Sit at my right hand, till I make your enemies your footstool.' By combining these two statements, we have an angelic man-figure who is sitting at the right hand of our Father. These two theological ideas entwined and became a statement for Christian eschatology (doctrine of 'last things,' i.e., the return of Christ, the final judgment, the Kingdom of God, the glorified human body, and the prospect of eternal life). Of note, in Aramaic, the 'Son of God' phrase translates into 'a human figure'."

Jesus officially began His ministry with a baptism ministered by John the Baptist in the River Jordan, during the reign of Emperor Tiberius (Mt 3:13–17). Thus, this event had to have occurred sometime between 27–29 C.E., with the most probable date being 28/29 C.E., because John the Baptist was calling for repentance and baptizing in the 15th year of Tiberius. Luke 3:23 states that Jesus was thirty years old when He began His public ministry. Based upon recorded trips (eighty-five percent walking, fifteen percent boating) healings in named towns, conversations with specified persons (date of their life) during a festival (timing of the season), it appears that Jesus's ministry lasted three years. As further proof, John's Gospel mentions incidents that occur over several Passovers, allowing us to view Jesus within the framework of a three-year ministry. Thus, Jesus was more than likely crucified when only thirty-three years old. Three short years of ministry, yet with a message so powerful that it continues to change the world!

To do the work of His Father, Jesus needed men and women who would carry on after He left the world. The first called by Jesus were Andrew, Simon Peter, and John (John 1:35–42) in a place known as al Maghtas, once known as Bethany beyond the Jordan, in early Autumn, 26 C.E.

On the heels of this event, Jesus called Philip and Nathanael (John 1:43–51). These disciples were simple fishermen (Simon Peter, Andrew, and John), a budding scholar (Nathanael), and a horse breeder (Philip) from the region of Galilee.

A question often wondered is, *"Why common folk? Why not have chosen among learned and reputable leaders?'* But the question should have been: *"Why would political or religious leaders who already lead the masses with skill, knowledge, manipulation, and accomplishments leave behind their world of fame, money, and power?"* If they already knew everything and possessed what they wanted, of what interest would it be for them to become followers after an itinerant rabbi? Jesus answered this question in Matthew 6:19–24 when He spoke on accumulating the treasures of the earth, and the impossibility of serving two masters. Due to the lack of change among the Palestinian leaders, we can state that Jesus's words of wisdom fell upon closed minds, frozen hearts, and ears that did not hear.

No, Jesus called the ordinary folk, the very people who needed to hear His words of earthly and eternal wisdom. These men and women were mostly the commoners, those comprising the majority of the uneducated, untrained, and unskilled in first-century Palestine. Their religious knowledge would have come from childhood teachings and worship services. Given the state of increased laws, those clarifications and modifications that further extended Moses's Ten Commandments and the Book of the Covenant (Exodus 20:22–23, 33) into confusing rules to follow daily, the ordinary people (*'am ha'artez*) appeared to have blended their religion's rules and regulations and everyday life into a workable and satisfying system. Blending was an act out of necessity, not out of disdain. Farmers who supported and supplied the religious and middle-class population worked by the sun and the seasons. They could not stop and travel to the Temple, but they did stop and kneel on the dirt and say their daily prayers. In all ways, the *'am ha'artez* gave Jesus His grassroots foundation.

Then what happened? What turned hardworking people of the earth into wisdom-filled crusaders? Acts 4:13 states that when the crowd "saw the boldness of Peter and John and perceived that they were uneducated and ordinary men, they were amazed and recognized them as companions of Jesus." As word spread of the happenings of Pentecost and the Resurrection, and witnessing the changes in Jesus's Apostles, Disciples, and Followers, realization grew that what was being freely offered had nothing to do with the world as they knew it, but everything to do with promise, betterment, and a life of meaning. In other words, a New Life. The miracle of transformation is available to anyone who raises their hand and says, "*I will follow.*" Jesus's New Life Resurrection continues, bettering this life with the promise of future wonders stretching into life everlasting.

Jesus chose His first group of twelve Apostles, those men whom He would teach and train. Once chosen, everything about their lives changed, for the demand for concentration was immense. They lived with Jesus day and night, leaving His side only after they began their missions of preaching and healing. His second group, known as Disciples, were young men who left family, friends, and jobs and traveled as Jesus's constant companions. Jesus taught them, and the Apostles added to their lessons. The Disciples used their new learnings to walk among the crowds who gathered to hear Jesus talk but failed to comprehend fully Jesus's meanings. The Disciples commonalty with the crowds aided in understanding Jesus's sometimes complex parables. Disciples followed Jesus's teachings—just as Disciples do today, teaching others and living out Jesus's New Life. A third group were the Followers. They maintained family and employment, traveling to hear Jesus whenever He was nearby. The demands upon their lives were enormous, yet their desire for the abiding Faith keep them seeking. A fourth group soon appeared. Startling, shocking, unbelievably, Jesus welcomed The Women. He included them in His ministry on equal terms with the men—even to the unheard point of teaching them!

People flocked to hear the words of Jesus. They rushed to Him for healing, a healing of the physical, and healing of the soul. Jesus offered hope, encouragement, and guidance. Most of all, Jesus gave them love. This love had no strings. It is as though He said to each individual personally, *"Listen to My words and change your life—or not. I will continue to love you unconditionally."*

In this moment of history, Jesus was a speaker to the Jewish people. They had no one on their side for their religious rites, rituals, and their 'One God' worship set them apart from the rest of the world's civilizations. Gone were their prophets who spoke for God, their seers, and sages. Rivalling Parthians and Romans wanted to rule them, own them. Laws and taxes had them trapped. Out of their ranks came Jesus, a devout, dedicated, loyal, obedient servant, who was willing and able to fill the void. His words of truth, guidance, and promise, and His loving, healing touch can be found and experienced over and over through the prayer Jesus spoke and offered to all.

Our Lord's death was cruel, perpetuated by fearful people. In the minds of the Temple hierarchy and the ruling Romans, Jesus was a political insurrectionist. He was a religious, political, economic, and societal subversive who called upon them to change their ways of leadership and administration. Where is righteousness, the fairness in Jesus's death? He asks that no one goes to bed hungry, and women be treated, not as property but as equals. Jesus asks for taxes to be reasonable, and attitudes toward classes be not about money but based upon a respectful assessment. He asks for forgiveness of self and for all others. Jesus asks us to help those in harm's way. Jesus simply asks that what is of 'good' be done, and what is 'ungodly' turned away. *"Pray,"* says Jesus, *"for OUR Father awaits the offering of our hearts, minds, and souls."* From these offerings will come the blessings this life has to give. We always begin with prayer.

Jesus the Prayerer Teaches Us

Our Lord's goals for His ministry were vastly ambitious as He wanted to offer life everlasting by:

- Opening a path for every individual to have an intimate relationship with God.
- Teaching the spiritual way of New Life to every soul.
- Healing physical, emotional, and mental pain.
- Instilling a love of Earth by showing and explaining nature's glorious offerings.
- Creating respect for all that lives.
- Demonstrating a better way to live through education, training, and equality for all.
- Reinforcing respect for legal laws and the societal need to obey them.
- Learning to live without undue mourning or regret.
- Instilling a love of be-ing via the teachings of forgiveness of oneself, neighbors, and enemies.

How is this possible, even probable? Jesus grew up in an ordinary Jewish environment where His family followed the Hebrew traditions of their Faith. Jesus attended the local synagogue for worship and study. Jesus debated *Halakhah* and *Haggadah* [aka *Aggadah*] with His elders. These are difficult subjects, and it is awe-inspiring to picture Jesus standing before adults who had studied the topics for decades. *Halakhah* alone means rabbinic issues discussed in the realm of reality and literalism, usually translated as 'Jewish Law,' which encompasses moral character and spiritual discipline. *Haggadah* means 'narrative,' as the stories chosen for study contain *Halakhah* topics, wherein students search for the human element worthy of imitation.

Debate was considered the greatest of all learning and teaching tools and, thus, used as part of normal conversation. Jesus readily debated with community Elders throughout the land, and with the great Temple and Sect teachers. The New Testament tells us that these holy men were impressed with the knowledge and wisdom from one so young. On the other hand, those destined to become rabbis studied—hard, six consecutive days every week, while volunteering their services for Sabbath worship. So, while Jesus's intelligence was undoubtedly that of supragenius, the amount of time in study, and then again, study through debate—all the while maintaining family and trade involvements—made His lifestyle comparable with the rabbi students. Or was it?

Let us take a moment and step into the mind of Jesus. Two books, along with your author's lifetime of study into our Lord's connection with Father, lead this discussion. The books are *The Mind of Jesus* by William Barclay and *Four Portraits, One Jesus* by Mark L. Strauss. We begin with the one passage from Barclay that first opened the door to understanding Jesus's first (maybe) encounter with the wrongness of a boxed-in Faith.

There was a thrill in the mind of the boy, Jesus, as he saw the gleaming Temple ahead, and as he climbed Mount Sion with the Passover pilgrims, singing, as generations of pilgrims had sung: 'I was glad when they said to me, Let us go to the house of the Lord.' (Ps. 122:1) He was sure that the Passover was going to give him the greatest experience in his life." And it was, but not in the way that our Lord expected. First to be sacrificed were the Passover lambs in the Temple court. Barclay mentioned how one part of the killed lamb, its blood, belonged to God. Think of the hundreds of thousands of worshippers standing in the Temple, watching as one priest slits the throat of while another catches a bowl of blood, and another priest passes the bowl along the altar. Imagine the pitiful cries of the lambs, the blood pouring out of the neck of the lambs, the smell of the blood from thousands of lambs, one for each person celebrating Passover, and spilt blood falling onto the marble squares causing the floors to be slippery. As Barclay noted, The Temple had "the atmosphere of a vast slaughterhouse and butcher's shop"—that is what Jesus saw. And in the mind of the young Jesus there arose the beginning of a great disillusionment" (pages 4–5).

With over 400,000–500,000 pilgrims attending Passover, it is reasonable to believe that half that number of lambs, meaning over 250,000 lambs, were slaughtered in a ritual unworthy to their Maker. In the scroll so dearly loved and read from daily, did everyone fail to note David's observation in Psalm 50:9–11: "I [Yahweh] will not accept a bull from your house, or goats from your folds. For every wild animal of the forest is mine, the cattle on a thousand hills. I know all the birds of the air, and all that moves in the field is mine." (NRSV) In other words, why would Creator God desire any creatures' death through sacrifice?

As your author contemplates Jesus's disgust as He stood there in the middle of the scene of thousands of innocent cries vocalizing their fear and horror, the thought of war arose, especially since I had a military husband during the Vietnam conflict. We humans so believe in the righteousness of our actions. During WWII, the Allies believed God was on their side. As did the U.S.A., the U.S.S.R., England, Poland, France, Africa, and all the other warring countries in between. When France fought Spain, God was believed to be on both sides. When England fought the Colonists, God was thought to be with both their nations.. It has always been this way. As Jesus stood in the middle of spilled blood, so our Christian soldiers have stood in the battlefields, wondering what the blood clotting their boots had to do with the love of God, or with being His Disciples? Maybe they asked the same question Jesus did— was there no way to stop this slaughter, for does not all living creatures belong to our Father? Neither the lambs nor soldiers dying in the battlefields have any say over their death. Do these scenes have anything to do with the Will of our Father?

Luke 2:41–49 adds the story of Jesus debating with the Temple rabbis. Tying this to the Temple Passover scene, Barclay adds his thought that Jesus went seeking answers on 'why sacrifice?' Surely, the Jewish Supreme Court, with their wise Sanhedrin judges, will know the necessity behind such an action. If not them, then *The Mishnah* (book of codified law) will provide answers. But this was not to be. Instead, in their wisdom, the learned rabbis were in full discussion on Sabbath law.

On page 6 of Barclay's book, he ties together Jesus' disgust over the slaughter of the innocent lambs to hearing the Sanhedrin judges debate. Barclay and just about every author who writes on the Sanhedrin court sessions express disappointment. The authors ask where are the judge's wisdom, their compassion for the people, their common sense in pronouncing reasonable and fair judgements? Are not their rulings to bring one closer to the Faith, their country more in line with the Will of God's Laws? No, and no. As an example, on this day is the on-going argument over the Sabbath Law. Actually, many, many Sabbath laws. If Jesus or anyone went to hear the Sanhedrin judges speak for justice on the Sabbath, they were greatly disappointed. One can find these arguments in the *The Mishnah* (*Shabbath* 6:2–5, 8; 8:4–6) where the minutiae of the law receives its day in court: Any type of work is forbid on the Sabbath. To carry is work. What defines work? If a cripple has a wooden leg, is he carrying a burden? What of a false tooth? Or what is he has nails in his sandals. One cannot pick up and stone and throw it for any reason. Nor may he write. We have read of other examples of where a man with a broken his leg must wait till the next day to receive treatment, and where an animal who fell into a ditch cannot lawfully be lifted out.

One can picture Jesus walking out of the court's chamber, shaking His head with disappointment in His heart. Jesus would not have heard God's teachings to the people, or the court's encouragement to follow along the commandments found in their covenants with God. When a person loves deeply, they seek reinforcement in the commitment of others who also proclaim that same love. This is true whether we speak of country, the country's law, religion, or one's religion. Jesus was bound to be discouraged with seeking righteousness from the leaders of His day. Little surprise that Jesus looked to the *'am ha'artez* for they, too, sought justice in Faith.

On the next page, Barclay comes close to ending his thought with, "He (Jesus) had suddenly discovered that the whole paraphernalia of sacrifice was a vast irrelevance, and the whole apparatus of the law a barrier to God." Two thousand years later, we are in the same position our Lord was in then. Church doors permanently closing, retired clergy rarely seen at worship services, young people not seeing the relevance in any religion; all the while, huge churches holding thousands of people sitting in comfortably padded chairs, listening to hired solos and 'making you feel good' sermons. The 'what have you done for me lately?' question and the lectures of 'your money makes this church viable' has diluted the feeling of the presence of the Trinity in our houses of worship. However, in times of disillusionment, we need to realize that intimacy with Father does not demand nor depend upon anything more than the connections we make through prayer. God will see to it that all other needs, those of engagement with faithful individuals, opportunities for study, and a more-profound satisfaction for the needs of the soul will receive His attention. Once we establish a connection with our Father, we are never left alone.

This is the most important lesson for us to learn. People who have lost everything, absolutely everything—from hurricane to fire, from war to concentration camp, have discovered they still possess the intuition, the desire to offer up a prayer and receive holy answers. What we need in prayer, we find. Our Lord taught us the value of petitionary prayer through example. It does not make any difference whether we are praying for spiritual growth or intercessory prayer.

In Matthew 7:7–8, Jesus gave us instructions on the 'how-to' of prayer, which your author coined the '3 KinGs of Prayer':

asK	=	you shall be receivinG
seeK	=	you shall be findinG
knocK	=	you shall be enterinG

Let us look at 'knocK, and you shall be enterinG,' as Jesus followed this prescription in the beginning and throughout His great mission. Before gathering His Apostles, Jesus used His time in further studies. He also developed the most authoritative, enduring, principled, and influential prayer life ever known, for the communication connection between Jesus and Father solidified into Oneness. What he learned in prayer prepared Him for His ministry. It was Strauss's study book that turned your author's mind to this insight. Strauss refers to Jesus as a powerful teacher, healer, and an exorcist throughout his book. What we know is that, as a child, Jesus did not leave the Temple area, return home with His parents, and immediate begin His ministry. No, life with our Father is never that easy. It would be years before Jesus was ready, years of praying, and listening of his Father's answers. Divine approval was given after John the Baptists' baptism of his cousin. God's voice from Heaven said, "This is my son, the Beloved, with whom I am well pleased" (Mt. 3:13–17). But what happened then? Did God give His Beloved Son an easy path to follow. No. Jesus' ministry would be one of hardship, paid, disappointment. Jesus found this out in the 40 days and 40 nights of Temptation as He fought his way through each extremely desirable temptation. Jesus prevailed and, in so doing, found the core of His determination. From this initiation, Jesus took His first step into messiahship.

The second step was in answering, "How then was He to fulfil the Will of God?" Jesus began as we all must begin. He asKed for guidance through prayer. Jesus already knew His life, His entire life, belonged to the Will of His Father. Jesus knew this because when thinking, when conversing, when sharing, when debating, when exploring—all with God, His Father—Jesus was at His apex of purpose and contentment. Jesus prayed all through His work as a carpenter assistant with Joseph, all through His studies in the Qumran community, and all through His relationship with His cousin, John the Baptist. Wherever Jesus traveled, whomever He was with, Jesus began and ended with prayer.

Why did He do this? Because Jesus was seeKing. To seek is to ask the questions. You cannot have one without the other. Immediately, help came to Jesus in the form of His community, the *Nazoreans/Nazarenes* (Mt. 2:23). All Hebrews knew themselves to be one united family, under the aegis of a remarkably strong Faith which had to prevail, down through the ages, against extraordinary odds. In no time, everyone in the community knew of Jesus and the Passover Temple rabbis' debate. One look on Jesus's face would have told them of His worry and frustration. His name would be in the daily prayers for the community. The Qumran compound of teachers and students continually prayed for one another, especially when receiving guidance on which steps to take into their future. John the Baptist and Jesus, meeting during the festivals when yearly family gatherings occurred, would have had many conversations on the 'when' for beginning their initial stage, the 'how-to' start the ministry, and the 'where' it should start. What an exciting time for Jesus, surrounded by supporters, teachers, and the synagogue rabbis who were always ready to engage, and eager to listen to, the young man with an unquenchable thirst for learning about the service of servanthood.

In every learning, in every opportunity, Jesus knocKed, for He wanted to learn in everything He could about our Father, about Heaven, about the Holy Spirit. He sought knowledge about combining Heaven and Earth so that all peoples would reap the reward of love, understanding, right living, fulfilment, and an abiding Faith that would lead all souls to His Father's heavenly Kingdom. Jesus knocked for the wisdom that would enable Him to reach every soul with lifesaving, life-eternal messages. Jesus asked nothing for Himself, and everything for everyone else—then and now.

Jesus knocked, wondering if He had learned enough. Was He ready? Is He hearing Father's voice 'now,' or is this His head saying what He wants, needs to hear? The first steps in His teaching ministry did not bode well for Jesus. Luke 4:14–21 explains, "Then Jesus (after the Temptation), filled with the power of the Spirit, returned to Galilee, and a report about him spread through all the surrounding country. He began to teach in their synagogues and received praise from everyone. When he came to Nazareth, where he had been brought up, he went to the synagogue on the Sabbath Day, as was his custom. He stood up to read, 'The Spirit of the Lord is upon me, because he has anointed me to bring good news to the poor. He has sent me to proclaim release to the captives and recovery of sight to the blind, to let the oppressed be free, to proclaim the year of the Lord's favor.' And he rolled up the scroll, gave it back to the attendant, and sat down. Then he began to say to them, 'Today this scripture has been fulfilled in your hearing.'" The people erupted in a fury. Was not Jesus the son of Mary and Joseph? How dare He proclaim Himself their Messiah!? And on went the discourse of disbelief.

Jesus tried a different door. This one was of signs and miracles, as seen when Jesus turned water into wine. His mother knew Jesus could perform miracles, or else she would not have asked Him to 'do something' at the Cana wedding (John 2:1–11). However, we have no idea what Jesus might have done before the water/wine display. In a way, this sign seems almost inconsequential when comparing the long-distance healing of the royal official's son in Capernaum in John 4:46–54, or healing with a touch the paralytic at Bethesda in John 5:1–15, or raising his friend, Lazarus from the dead, in John 11:1–45.

Yet, more was needed, for bodily ills and emotional trauma were of this world, but inside the mind, a darker region required help. Therefore, Jesus knocKed again and mercifully received the wisdom to fight what the New Testament identifies as the 'demons' who bring havoc upon a person's thought-processes. First-century physicians did not know about chemical imbalances, diseases of the brain, or shock from trauma. Mental illness was a mystery the people explained by attributing the illness to curses, demons, or the Devil, Satan. Jesus did not even try to explain otherwise. He never gave explanations or details for any of His cures. He simply, quietly cured so that the person could go on to live a healthy, wholesome, and meaningful life.

At this point, Jesus had enough standing in the land that He could travel the countryside with His Apostles and Disciples, picking up Followers and Listeners who craved His words and healings. The ministry was now in full swing with all the necessary tools available. Each day was packed full of travel, sermonizing, curing, speaking with individuals, and teaching. From sunrise to sunset, Jesus worked to fulfil those ambitious goals. He did so with prayer every step of the way.

Based upon the biblical renderings of Jesus's prayer life, we can readily image Jesus opening His eyes from sleep and whispering, "Father." God answers, "Jesus," and Jesus immediately rolls onto His knees and begins to pray. This example is set for us, as Mark 1:35 states, Jesus prayed first thing in the morning. How could He do otherwise? The very origin of Jesus's name means 'prayer.' In the ancient Semitic script (from which flows Aramaic and Hebrew) are the letters of His name 'Y S U.' With the necessary vowels added, these three letters translate into *Yeshau* or *Yeshu*. In Biblical Hebrew, this name reads as '*Yehoshuah*.' Thus, the very name of Jesus means the prayer: 'Yahweh saves,' 'God saves,' 'He will save,' and 'Yahweh is salvation.' Every time Jesus heard His name spoken, He thought of what it meant for His New Life message, *Salvation through Prayer*.

Look at Jesus's mind as divided: part in prayer and part in action, or part in Heaven and part on Earth. This may sound strange, but it really is not. Relationships require communication. The more meaningful the conversations, the more intimacy grows. Over time, the prayer bond becomes unbreakable, a habit set for life. In reading the Gospels, one begins to realize that the question, 'When does Jesus pray?' is never asked. Instead, 'When is Jesus not praying?' circulates in wonderment. People soon realized that whenever the Apostles and Disciples were out among them, teaching, feeding, answering questions, Jesus was nowhere in sight; their rabbi was off praying.

When Jesus returned, He was rejuvenated. Teachers and physicians can attest to their profession's high demands and how mind and body weary and stresses. They might take naps. But Jesus energized through prayer. He returned to the mission purposefully, having communicated thoughts, questions, insights, and problems to The One who always listened and always responded. I have this fanciful vision that when Jesus was overly tired, He rested in the arms of our Father, awakening to the wonderment of His mission, and how life-changing His ministry had become to those who came to Him with an open mind and a willing heart.

The prayers of Jesus were spontaneous. The Gospels do not record that Jesus ever stopped at set times to pray, probably because the connection between Him and Father was always open. This is what is meant by Jesus's mind being divided, half for earthly concerns and a half for divine intercourse. With time, this happens to prayerers. The more one prays, that is, speaks to Father, the less one speaks to self. No regulated prayers are recorded as being spoken by our Lord. Still, we must seriously doubt that Jesus broke with tradition and never uttered the known themes found within the Shema, the 18 Benedictions, and the morning, afternoon, and evening prayers. Jesus would have offered up the Psalms of Praise with great delight. He would have shed tears when offering the prayers of Kaddish.

From the themes within the daily, fasting, and festival prayers, and His conversations with Father, Jesus realized that certain features of prayer appeared persistently, not all at the same time, but when the need approached. Other elements were of 'function,' while others were of 'emotion' in content.

Sometimes, Jesus's prayer was short. His need to communicate with Father involved an issue not requiring detail or time. Sometimes, Jesus would pray for hours, even throughout the night. With these two facts in mind, please realize that the following is not a 'how-to' step-by-step prayer list. It is more of 'tidbits' for thought, an encouragement to stay connected with The One who loves you most in all the world.

Functional Prayer Elements, Part 1

PRAISE begins our prayer, for the opportunity to speak with Father. We praise God for creation, our beautiful world, and even for the hunger in our souls that is fed through our communication with Him. We thank God with praise.

THANKSGIVING is next, as we thank Father for the blessings of our life, for the privilege of being able to speak with Him, and for loving us unconditionally—the greatest gift we could ever receive.

INTERCESSION holds an exceptionally high honor, for asking on behalf of another is an act of compassion and love for one's neighbor. Please, do not feel you need to know the individual for whom you are praying. You do not.

There are many people in many situations requiring our prayers. Unknown to you are the prayers for the sick, those facing an operation, or are wrongly imprisoned, those facing bankruptcy, or those who are hungry or frightened. Offer your prayers for them.

For those whom you know need your prayer, please picture him or her in your mind. Lay your hands upon his or her head. Pray. Imagining your prayer adds clarity to your meaningful words. Yes, even laypeople pray for others with the laying on of hands. Our Lord touched others when in prayer for them, and we are to follow in His footsteps.

ALMSGIVING, for we are our 'brother's keeper' (Genesis 4:1–13). This almsgiving is first given in prayer as we remember those least fortunate, and we finish with our offering to them. This commitment to helping others is made not only in coin but in visitation, in volunteering, and in the delivery of food and clothes, toys, and over-the-counter medicines. Opportunities exists for almsgiving, and we must not overlook the need.

PETITION requests include pieces of intercession and almsgiving, for we are requesting our Father to remember our prayers for those in need.

o The petition also gets extraordinarily personal, for we seek our Father's direct response for those mentioned in our appeal. Here in prayer, we become specific: names, places, timing, reason, and hopeful outcome.

OBEDIENCE TO THE WILL OF GOD is where we go next as we give our minds over to our Maker. We pray that Father will consider our requests' specificity, knowing we offered it with our limited understanding of the problem.

Our prayer has not been without emotion. Rather than run or hide from our feelings, it is essential to embrace our feelings and act on them. We do not hide, we persevere. We do not escape behind pride but humble ourselves before our Father. We do what we must to find the path to forgiveness. If necessary, we can depend upon God's help and patience. We need to forgive for this leads to the path of total repentance, as which point we the return to a wholesome relationship with our Father.

Emotional Prayer Elements, Part 2

PERSEVERANCE is a necessity, as the desire or the situation or the facts change. Letting Father know that the intent, the need, is prevalent in keeping the issue alive as it stretches its importance.

HUMILITY is a necessity. Who are we, and what impact do our problems have in a world of chaos, wars, starvation, and all the other horrors we humans perpetrate on one another?

FORGIVENESS is a heavy burden. We know why forgiveness of self and others is necessary. We do not want to carry around the guilt, the shame, that terrible sense of uncomfortableness because we are not doing what our Father is Heaven is asking of us.

Still, it does not always help to understand the need, or its helpfulness in our spiritual growth, or the freedom offered when no longer feeling the ugliness of anger and hatred. We are trapped in a black hole. It hurts to forgive. The darker the deed, the more painful the hurt. When the heart is in pain, the mind wants to shut down. Nerves tingle and swelling of limbs occur. Acute trauma brings onslaught to thought. Feelings numb themselves into oblivion. Barriers rise. Self-protection.

And here comes our Lord saying, "Forgive, forgive."

Sometimes, your author feels that our Lord simply asks for too much. Give me the person who talked badly about me, or the individual who stole my money. They will have my forgiveness. But for those causing life-changing, immense pain, I have said, "Father, I love you—but you are asking the impossible." When speaking these words, I expect the battle to begin. Instead, I feel—honestly feel—our Father's loving touch.

Our loving God has patience along with great understanding. God knows our struggles. Our Father appreciates that the pace of our travels on our spiritual journey may not be as quick or as easy as we hoped. So be patient with yourself. Do not allow others to lay the burden of absolute and immediate forgiveness on you right now. Trust in prayer. Ask for our Lord and the Holy Spirit to aid you in your quest to find forgiveness. Our Father, who loves us unconditionally, deeply, and who wants only the best for us, will surely approve of these actions. Pray, for this is according to the will of our Father.

REPENTANCE is essential. If we cannot say, "*I am wholeheartedly sorry,*" then why should our Father pay us any heed? Without genuine sorrow, we will repeat and repeat the same wrongdoing. We absolutely must recognize and accept our part in our action(s). Only sorrow, shame, and regret can lead to true repentance. And trust me on this: Father will know if we harbor an inkling of anger, a thought of revenge, or a desire for payback. If these emotions still exists, far better for us to pray for their eradication than pray with false repentance.

THANK YOU is a statement that comes from the heart for our Father has given us His listening ear and compassion and the understanding He extended toward us during the prayer. We say this before uttering 'Amen.'

Functional Prayer Elements, Part 3

We are not finished.

Prayer needs to be in two steps. We just completed the first step. We prayed.

Now, we listen.

o Stay where you are.
o Be still.
o Be quiet.
o Listen.
o Give yourself over.
o Go deep within.
o Listen.
o You will receive a reply.
o Sometimes, you will hear "Wait" or "No, not possible" because you are requesting something that cannot be undone.
o You might hear, "Speak more so that you understand more fully what you are asking."
o Harder to hear is, "Your forgiveness is not complete," or "Go and reconcile, and then come back to Me," or "You need to talk about this with your confessor/clergyperson/friend," etc.
o Best of all is to hear, "You have done well, my daughter/son." There are numerous responses our Father can make and does

make to us. Sadly, too many people have already returned their consciousness to daily activity.

Only after listening and receiving our guidance do we offer a statement of our obedience to the Will of our Father.

AMEN, AMEN, AND, AGAIN, AMEN! Terms of glory and pride, thanksgiving with smiles. Unconditional love blankets my life. I do not know about you, but I do know that I do not have unconditional love from another human. Yes, I have love in my life. Husband and friends offer a mighty supply of this needed substance for living. But unconditionality comes from The One who created my soul! My very existence came about from He who blew His breath into the particles of my soul and offered me the gift of life. So I say, with all the too many flaws, and wrongdoings, and missteps, I offer my praise, thanksgiving, and my promise to do better, to be a better person.

Jesus's Teachings on Prayer

A remarkable gift concerning prayer is that it can take place at any hour, in any location. You can be in seclusion or a crowded room. Jesus prayed while alone (Luke 9:18), while in the wilderness-desert (Luke 5:15–16), and Jesus prayed while in the mountains (Matthew 14:23).

On the first day of His ministry, Jesus prayed (Mark 1:35–38). He would not have dreamed of beginning a new job without praying first! For those in management, take note: Jesus prayed before choosing His Disciples (Luke 6:12–16).

Jesus's healings were accompanied by prayer as our Lord was fulfilling our Father's desire in what He needed Jesus to be doing in His ministry. Knowing the importance of this, Jesus wanted God with Him every step of the way! Take note of how Jesus prayed when healing the leper in Luke 5:12–16. The miracle of the feeding of the 5,000 was accompanied by prayer (Mark 6:37–44).

When Jesus asked, *"Who do you say I am?"* Peter confessed his faith in Him as the Messiah. And Jesus prayed a prayer of thanksgiving upon hearing Peter's statement (Mark 8:27–30). Not surprisingly, Jesus was at prayer when His Apostles asked for a teaching on how to pray (Luke 11:1). Upon hearing their request, our Lord gladly informed Father of this good news through prayer and immediately began to teach them.

One essential item to remember about Jesus and His prayer life is that He prayed when the need or desire was upon Him. He waited for no man. In reading Mark 1:37, we see that Jesus sought seclusion and prayed while knowing others were searching for Him. The need to be alone with Father was paramount. Maybe God had been calling Jesus as God called to Moses and David. We do not know. What we do know is that when our Father summons, we respond.

Why? Out of a need to please or hear about our next life's chapter. Like Jesus, we want to communicate with God throughout the good, bad, and in between times. Sometimes we even cry out for Father's immediate attention. He is always with us. We are never disappointed. And this is why—when summoned—we respond, hopefully with passion. Our eagerness will always signal God that our connection to Him is as vital as the time we have been allotted on this earth. For Christians, 'prayer' and 'life' are partners. We spoke earlier of Jesus's divided mind. Well, ours will be divided as well. The more we pray, talk to our Father, the more He becomes an integral part of our daily activities. Father knows everything about me because I tell all. I even once told Him the joke about the rabbi, priest, and plumber. A full burst of rolling thunder was the response! Need I say more?

Aside from the lightness of this conversation, there is an utmost seriousness to prayer, to our partnership of the life and the eternity we have with Father. The good times can be shared—these joys and the laughter. We do this sharing with the knowledge that dark happenings do occur. It happened to your author. When the physical pain started, Healer Jesus was by my side. When my acceptance into seminary was in process, the Holy Spirit guided the way. Faith, this glorious entity who brings essence and substance into our lives, is everything. And I pray it is, or will be, for you.

The aging process and facing death are huge struggles, each in their own way. When suffering from a disease or have been in a bad accident, we suspect, even know, we are dying. We may accept the news and pray for comfort. Or we may fight and try to change the outcome. Or curl up in trepidation. Or attempt to change fate with alcohol and drugs. It need not be this way. Again, turn to the model offered by our Lord. As He showed us how to live, He also showed us how to die:

- At the Mount of Transfiguration, Jesus prayed for courage as He contemplated His death. How His heart must have been breaking. The years of study, the Apostles' mission training, the public teachings, and, in just three short years, it ends. Was it enough time? It takes no great imagination the words of Jesus's prayer to Father (Luke 9:28–29).
- Jesus prayed for strength before entering Jerusalem for what He knew would be the last time (Luke 19:29–44), the people He loved, the city He would never see again as a free man.
- In the Upper Room, he gathered the Apostles and prayed with them (John 13:21–32). His breaking of the bread and the drinking of the wine was a gift of remembrance to Him. He refreshed and strengthened their bodies to carry on His great teachings of the New Life.
- Three times Jesus prayed in the Garden of Gethsemane for strength and courage to face what lay ahead (Mark 14:32–42). He asked His friends, the Apostles, to join Him in prayer. They fell asleep instead, not because they did not love Jesus but because they could not face what Jesus told them was going to happened. So, they hid in sleep and suffered the consequences of conscience for the rest of their lives. Jesus did not have the choice of sleep. What is the value of sleep when one is facing death, a cruel, inhuman death? Instead, as Jesus deepened His

prayer to Father, begging for release, the release given to Him was the outpouring of blood in His sweat (Luke 22:44). *Thy Will Be Done*. Do not pray for what cannot be changed.

- Jesus would die on the cross. He was without family or friends, as they were too afraid of the soldiers to pray at His feet. Our Lord gave His last prayer for humanity, *"Father, forgive them, for they know not what they do"* (Luke 23:33–49).

- With His last breath, Jesus offered up what your author considers a most beautiful and meaningful finish to His human experience. I sincerely pray I am capable of imitating His last thoughtful statement, *"Father, into thy hands, I commend my spirit"* (Luke 23:46 KJV).

The Importance of Language

GROWTH OF LANGUAGE & DEVELOPMENT CHART
© by BC Crothers and Lee Jones

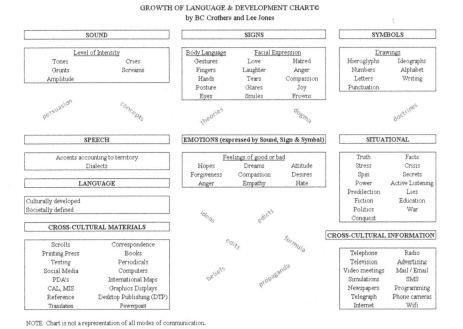

NOTE: Chart is not a representation of all possible modes of communication.

The above chart speaks to the three elements necessary for speech and language to work: sounds, signs, and emotions. Why is this important? Because without our language, we would never have been able to communicate our desires, especially the desire for a Faith, a belief system that could guide us. Since the beginning of time, we humans have wanted to reach out to one another, make that all-important connection called 'intimacy.' The love and mutual respect we have for one another are humanity's grease on the wheels of growth. From

135

growth derives attitude, motivation, ideas, inventions, and exploration. The list is endless because human possibilities are endless. In short order, humanity has gone from cave dwelling to cities populated by millions. Before the next generation of elders die, we might well be seeing a colony of explorers, scientists, inventors, agriculturists, electricians, and others who are all needed in building a new world on a new planet. With them, they will take our languages. What will their language sound like?

Two articles on bitstream, *Importance of Language in Society* and *sociologydiscussion.com* speak to language development. One joint point is how neither sound, nor tone, gestures, signs, not even speech, can stand alone. For communication to be successful, all elements must be in play. The one exception needing to be included are those deaf. Their communication depends upon a sign language with facial gestures and bodily reactions. Yet, as we read this, we need to understand that language is not static. The language spoken in our youth is not identical because old words die out and new terms are invented. The evolution of one's native language will speed up the changes in worldwide languages. For example, take the mobile technology of the Short Message Service, an SMS language consisting of texting instantly through the air, utilizing the Internet, cell phones, and chat forums, all instantaneously in the cosmic timeline. How could this have happened so rapidly?

Language is also broken down into categories. All societies have taboo words that forbid an expression not tolerated by its people. Another category is how unique term usage can be found isolated within the labs of science, medicine, and developmental laboratories specializing in electronics, technologies, and space-travel equipment. New words and slogans receive international popularity overnight when they resonate across cultures and societies, hitting on an emotional truism found within the human psyche. Think advertising, the Nike slogan, 'Just Do It.' Think journalism and political oratory, 'Fake News.'

Consider not only the rapidity and the duplicity of language but what happens to the all-important need to share feelings or transmit a scream, a laugh. Oh, wait. We have little cave drawings identified as today's emojis (electronic ideographs) of open mouths, clapping hands, tears rolling down cheeks, and smiley faces! Will this be enough? Can an emoji tell you of my innermost thoughts?

We will continue to have speed and language shortcuts. We will continue to find means for emotional communication. We also must deal with language fallacies. People lie, manipulate, control, and even destroy with language. Propaganda, especially that of calculated misinformation, false or deliberately incorrect arguments, will continue to be used to sway and convince. Falsely planted news tied to an intentionally cropped photo can ruin lives or start a war. Language, particularly spiced with ethnic terms and morality clauses, can continue to be at the core of civilization or can turn humans into unthinking, uncontrollable mobs. Yes, all true. But, in the long run, we can trust the authenticity of language. Can we not?

No, we cannot. We have the history of speeding through language development, which is either running to or running from international trade, economic ventures, wars, migrations, and mixed marriages between races and nationalities and religions. Nothing is static, and nothing stays the same. Change is growth. Change is progress. Even the language of history changes.

The difficulty is far greater than *"history is written by the victors"* (Churchill). One must deal with the fact that languages come and go. Cultural changes and society's misunderstanding, or misinterpretation of the language, can change a country's boundary lines. Between 2000 and 2019, *en.wikipedia.org* notes that thirty-three countries have fought border conflicts. Misunderstanding or misinterpretation problems too often derive from translation difficulties.

Our Holy Bible is a perfect example. It has been written in biblical Hebrew, Aramaic, Greek, Old Latin, in 'new' Latin, African, Italian, both Old Syriac and the Syriac Vulgate, in 'mixed' text, the Thebaic

Version, and in the European text. Twelve renditions in twenty centuries, while not counting the multiple versions done mostly in English, with new editions produced continually in *King James Version, New King James Version, New American Standard Bible, New Revised Standard Version, New International Version, and English Standard Version*. The list names only a fraction of the 450 translations of the Holy Bible into English. Also, we should not overlook book-company editions, such as *The HarperCollins Study Bible, The New Oxford Annotated Bible with Apocrypha, Zondervan Study Bible, the Holman Christian Standard Study Bible*, or specialized books like the *Archaeological Study Bible*. Nor must we overlook Holy Bible translations written in freestyle of individuals, such as E.H. Peterson and W.W. Wangerin, Jr. Take this lengthy mixture of translations, choose a single word, and then follow it through the maze of interpretations. You embark upon a journey of amazement and confusion.

It is amazing how the history of the Palestinian language revolved around the Aramaic, Hebrew, and Greek languages, both in oral tradition and written scrolls. Christian Jewish Apostles, Disciples, family members, friends, and Followers of our Lord wrote bits and pieces of His life and deeds according to their memories. The next generation added what they had been told. Jesus's life, ministry, and death were written down in Hebrew, with only a few Aramaic phrases kept intact, such as His death cry *"Eli, Eli, lema sabachthani?"* ("My God, my God, why have you forsaken me?") in Matthew 27:46. Aramaic also appeared in the sign over the head of our dying Lord. Pilate had written in Latin, Greek, and Aramaic, 'The King of the Jews' (John 19:20).

The scrolls that contained these stories were copied, recopied, and recopied. Who can tell how many of the four Gospels were rewritten? Stories are told of church scribes and priests who could not read and relied on only what they saw. Other stories tell of scribes changing biblical text and writing notes in the margins that were later copied into the verses, thinking they were part of the corrected text. Handheld copies would make their way into foreign lands by missionaries.

Ancient Hebrew gave way to Greek. Alexander the Great is credited with the spread of both the Greek culture and its language. Though he failed to conquer the world, he did succeed in making Greek the common, spoken, and written language. From the first century to the beginning of the third century, the Church of Rome's liturgy and literature was all in the Greek language. But, like most languages, Greek lost its dominance. Latin became more appealing to the Roman Church. The change in emphasis in the language may have begun the schism between the Roman Church and the Greek Eastern Orthodox Church, but the fierce disagreements over doctrine completed the schism; that is, in this case, a permanent break over divisions in doctrine.

Christianity in Rome was under the domain of the Roman Church. The church's hierarchy, along with the cardinals and archbishops could read, but only a few priests. The recorded first Roman clerical institution, according to *newadvent.org*, began with Cardinal Capranica in 1417 with thirty-one clerics. Officially, the first seminary only began during the Council of Trent (1545–1563). Traditionally, a priest-in-training simply repeated what he had learned from the teachings of his mentor, usually an older priest. Congregants could not read. Asking questions about what was being taught was discouraged. This was not a time of Jesus's religious freedom. Jesus's entire ministry strove to free people from manmade dogma. His encouragement was and is to speak to God the Father and follow His ministry's teachings into the New Life.

Jerusalem has a different Christian history than Rome, for it had a mixture of its Christian Hebrews called 'the brethren,' and its synagogues were strongly under the Hellenistic influence. The brethren continued to speak Hebrew, but it too had changed. The language began with Paleo-Hebrew, travelled onto Biblical Hebrew, and developed into the scholarly Mishnaic Hebrew. Into the mix was still a scattering of Aramaic, no longer being spoken, and without the *kotzo shel yod* (every jot and tittle; that is, its pronunciation marks), making it almost impossible to read. This exact difficulty occurred later with the reading and understanding of the text written in Biblical Hebrew.

Considering the issues with language, just how much of the Holy Bible can be trusted to be truthful or accurate? The book is filled with myth, allegory (symbolic stories), legend, fable, folktale, fiction, incorrect dating, and parables. It is also filled with mystery, wonderment, 'what ifs,' fascination, surprise, speculation, shock, disbelief, puzzle, and warning.

What the Holy Bible also contains is valuable teachings about life, how to live and die, offers examples on the intricacies of humans, and tells of the indomitable human spirit. One reads biographies about those persons who succeeded, those who failed, those who were destroyers, and those who were heroes.

Inside the Holy Bible, we find the glory of Heaven, the delight of angels, the abundant creativeness and love of our Creator, the healing and loving compassion of our teacher and savior Jesus, and become acquainted with the Holy Spirit who shelters and protects us in ways we will never know about. In other words, we learn about the elements of Faith, how to live them, and how not to be swayed by unfaithfulness.

All the lessons from the Holy Bible are not fiction, nor are they fact. People make a mistake thinking that it is, but the readings therein contains mixtures of possibilities and warnings. It is a story about people attempting to make sense of the world and their place in it. Actually, this is a very readable book about Seekers. The Holy Bible helps us understand the need to seek and to acknowledge the drive to discover the next steppingstone. The Holy Bible is for Soul-Seekers who want to know how one's spiritual journey fits into this thing we know as the 'Freewill Life.'

Pick up the Holy Bible; the translation does not matter. Discover your soul's journey inside its pages and enjoy the rest of your journey. Fall in love with this book called the Holy Bible, and I, your author, solemnly promises that what you hold in your hands will love you back.

Was the Lord's Prayer Spoken in Hebrew or Aramaic?

It is amazing how people can become so passionate and fixated after first formulating a hypothesis and then, from that point on, believing their hypothesis to be a fact! There are biblical scholars, theologians, clergy, historians, archaeologists, and lay theologians who have taken a stand—or side—on whether Jesus spoke His prayer in Hebrew, or was it Aramaic?

For decades, your author pulled quotes from hundreds of readings done on the Lord's Prayer. From those statements, the following chart was created to show just how compelling each side, and each argument, can be. No references were ever kept due to each quote being found in numerous books. The idea here is to offer an array of the opinions.

HEBREW	ARAMAIC
Most parts of the Old Testament	I do not believe four verses make up two
were written in 98 percent	Percent of the OT. The four Aramaic
Hebrew.	Verses include: 2Kings 18:26, Ezra 4:7, Isaiah 36:11, and Daniel 2:4. (truthonlybible.com)
The Law and the Prophets were	An interpreter translated the Law and the
Both written in Hebrew and in	Prophets into Aramaic during the
Hebrew.	Service.
Formal, corporate (forming one	Private prayers were said in the Aramaic
body of many individuals)	Prayers language.
were given in Hebrew. The ordinary people of Palestine could understand simple prayers said in Hebrew.	
The Shema (the confession of	The Shema could be recited in the
Faith in the one God and God's	Synagogues and the Jerusalem Temple in
commandments) was written in	Any language.
Hebrew.	
The 18 Benedictions were written	The Mishnah stated that the 18
in Hebrew.	Benedictions could be recited in any language.
The Morning Prayer and the	The oldest parts of the Kaddish prayer
Evening Prayer were written in	Were written in Aramaic.
Hebrew. However, Morning Prayer	However, this is a corporate prayer.
and Evening Prayer are private	
prayers – not corporate.	
The communal prayers of the	The Gospel of Luke used the Aramaic
Dead Sea Scrolls are written in Hebrew	term 'sin,' written as *ḥōb*. Interestingly, Latin continued the term's original meaning of wrongdoing by defining
Jesus carried out His ministry among	sin' to mean 'guilty'.
a mostly Jewish populace, but not much	
to the Rabbis, Doctors of the Law,	Jesus would have given the prayer in
Pharisees, Temple priests, Highpriest	Aramaic because it was easier for the
and upper-class Palestine citizens. They	*'am ha'aretz*, the common people, to

could speak in Hebrew, but not all	understand and most of his ministry was
could read the Hebrew script. Jesus	carried out primarily among these people
would have spoken His Lord's Prayer in Hebrew to them. However, within a decade, people of all classes were beginning to listen.	

The Beginnings of Christianity

Jesus is the founder of the Christian Faith, but He did not physically build its church. The last chapters of the four Gospels tell of Jesus's arrest, beatings, trial, more beatings, a second trial, the carrying of His cross to the site of the crucifixion, and the awful and traumatic death scene. But the Gospels do not end with our Lord's death—but with His continued life. Jesus had died, risen, and, in this time of His earthly Resurrection, walked among family members, Apostles, and friends.

Theologians and religious historians have basically come to an agreement on the sequence of events after Jesus rose from the tomb. Most Holy Bibles carry this information in its index areas. April 9 is an important date. The day began early with Peter and John at the now-empty tomb. After they left, Mary Magdalene arrived, shocked to find Jesus's body missing. Jesus came to show her He still lives. He then appears to other women.

In the afternoon of the 9th, Jesus appeared to Cleopas and his companion on the road to Emmaus. Throughout the day, those who saw or talked to Jesus hurried to find the Apostles. Witnesses told them what had occurred, but not all the Apostles believed them. (Doubting Apostle Thomas would have his own encounter with Jesus [John 20:24-29]). Later that evening, Jesus made His appearance to the Apostles present.

From April 10 to the 16th, there are no recordings of what transpired between Jesus and His Apostles or anyone else. Speculation holds to the tradition that Jesus was teaching the Apostles what they needed to know to carry on His ministry. Jesus had begun a mission of universal salvation where failure was not an option. After Jesus's teachings were concluded, He ascended. This happened 39 days after Easter Sunday. Thus, Ascension Day is the 40th day after Easter. In *gematria* (Jewish numerology), the number '40' represents a generation. The number's importance is also based upon the number of years Moses and his people travestied the desert, and the number of days and nights of the Noachian Flood. Your author has little doubt that the tears shed during our times of spiritual dryness matches these representations.

Why are the April dates important? Because when the time was approaching for Jesus to leave, He informed the Believers that He was not going to leave them alone, that they were never going to be alone again. The Acts of the Apostles, chapter 2, tells us about the happenings on the day of Pentecost. Consider this coincidence: in Jewish history, Pentecost is celebrated at the same time the Jewish people are celebrating Shavuot (Feast of Weeks). In Christian history, Pentecost is when Jesus presented the Holy Spirit to the people (Acts 2).

As the room full of people knelt in prayer, stating their belief in the Risen Lord aloud, the Holy Spirit came upon them, baptized them in Jesus's name, and, afterward, the newly formed Christians were never the same again. This is the way baptism and the Holy Spirit's blessing are supposed to have continued to this very day.

We do not know if Jesus ever informed the Apostles of the coming destruction of Jerusalem Temple, though He did hint at it with His 'three days' comparison with the Pharisees in John 2:18–21. Maybe the Apostles did not need to be told. The tensions between foreign and local leaders, the corrupt taxation system, the Teachers of the Law, and the Sanhedrin judges, who heard only their own thoughts, was only the beginning. The Pharisees told the 'am ha'artez only what they wanted them to hear, and the over-burdened populace had heard enough. They closed their ears to them, while opening their ears to one another to hear the whispers, "*Revolution!*"

You cannot blame the people. A caste-like social system existed between the Hellenized wealthy, the middle-class tradesmen, and the incredibly poor commoners. The culture was at a standstill, as even Hellenism had limited growth. Jewish physicians were not allowed to touch a human body, dead or alive, and their medical knowledge was extremely primitive compared to the surgeries and medical discoveries made by the Greeks. Nothing of great importance was being invented in first century Palestine. Anything new, such as material for clothing, came from abroad. As did spices. Ships and caravans brought the world to Palestine, and the people could see, smell, and hear what they were missing. The Zealot's cry of *"Freedom from the oppressors!"* gained in strength as more and more despairing people came to listen. The Apostles had less than forty years to build an enduring, life-changing ministry. (Here is the reality—and the promise—of our renewal process.)

The rise of the Christian Faith began with personal testimonies. Simon Peter preached to the crowds, offering testimonials to the character, power, healings, and teachings of our Lord. He was recognized as the head of the church, for all knew of Jesus's words, "Upon this rock, I will build my church." (Mt. 16:18) For all his human weaknesses, Peter was our rock. Herein lies the lesson for us all: weak Peter, troubled by his failure, unforgiving of self, continued to fulfil our Lord's need of him. He preached Jesus's word to the masses, won converts, baptized, healed, and proclaimed the Kingdom to those who patiently awaited the return of the Messiah.

The other Apostles followed suit. They discovered their strengths and went to work. Gospels and letters were written. Apostles preached for a while in Palestine, but most became missionaries, going into foreign lands. The Apostles left Palestine, for the Jewish people closed ranks and no longer recognized Jesus as their Messiah. In their eyes, He had been a fake, because the Kingdom had not immediately 'come'; the enemies had not been slaughtered at the gate. Jesus had told the Apostles to go to those wanting to listen, for all needed to hear. And they went.

The Apostles went with their memories, and they spoke in the oral tradition of their people. Oral presentations could be trusted, for it had 5,000 years of practice on which to rely. Inside an individual's memory, every bit of tribal history, travel, genealogy, battles, wars, verbal agreements, and family backgrounds existed. From laws to prayers, to generational family names to animal care, how to deliver a baby, and more were part of a person's knowledge and memory.

It was not the memories, or the travels, or old age that ended the Apostles' missionary journeys. Each Apostle, except for John the Beloved, met with martyrdom. Other men rose to take their places. The writing of the Gospels was written to meet the unique needs of their communities. These Gospels were copied and sent on to be used in other areas. The copies travelled far and wide, translated into dozens of languages. Jesus's mission statements were getting out into the world.

What one might find strange is that 'happy' stories about Jesus, the person, are not part of the Gospels' genre. Do not get me wrong. Tremendous experiences occurred, which, even today, have the power to bring us to our knees—in thanksgiving and in awe. But our Lord suffered. The moments of Jesus's happiness came when He talked with our Father, His group of Apostles, Disciples, Followers, and the crowds. Jesus laughed when with His friends.

The three years of ministry were years of preaching, teaching, sermonizing, healing, and praying. When engaged in ministry activities, we can feel His joy, that wonderful sense of purpose, the great love for life and all that live. Jesus's desire for spiritual freedom through solid connections with one another is apparent in His teachings. They show us how to be better, live better, discover our talent, work at our passion, enjoy the fruits of our labor, and develop into the person God created us to become. All this, from He who gives, heals, and loves unconditionally.

These were Jesus's 'happy' times. Yet in the narrations of our Lord's events, the Gospels offer a more telling truth. Jesus' life was beset by insults, denials, and rejections. Roman soldiers sent by Pilate, and Temple spies sent by Herod and the Sanhedrin were a constant. Jesus knew they were reporting back His every word, listening, waiting for that one word, one action for which the charge of treason, or sedition, or heresy would be made against him. These incidents were all reported in the Gospel chapters by people who had listened and learned Jesus's lessons, and they knew that only the truth would set us free. The Gospels were written to address problems the Christian community was experiencing. Though sameness in events occurred, the Gospels tell of unique situations which might be of help to the community, their leaders, and believers who were seekers of the way. For those three years, Jesus had to learn to walk the steppingstones of purpose and fulfillment with each step mixed with insult, hurt, and disbelief.

One strain runs through all four Gospels as the writings unveil the happenings of struggles, unhappiness, ridicule, shame, and the demands for answers from disbelievers and dangerous enemies. Our Lord was rejected by His own family members. Peter, whom He appointed head of His church, would deny Him three times. Judas Iscariot, an Apostle of His own choosing, betrayed Jesus to His enemies. The horrific and traumatic death scenarios of arrest, beating, trial, more beatings, second trail, carrying the cross to His crucifixion, and dying the humiliating death of a common criminal.

Why, why did this happen? Because of where we are today, my writing, your reading. The death of Jesus was not the end of this story. In actuality, the Resurrection is a continuation of the first steps Jesus took after answering to our Father, *"Thy will be done."*

Churches would be built for those who believed in our Lord's messages, as they wanted and needed to be with other Believers. Theologies and doctrines under the title 'Christology' (branch of theology dealing with the meanings of Jesus the Christ) would be developed in councils with priests and theologians all discussing Jesus's words. There were categories to discuss—more than mentioned but certainly on the issues of sin, forgiveness, repentance, redemption, human relationships, marriage, ethics, morals, salvation, Kingdom, Kingdom come, end of the world, life everlasting, eternity, and the importance of prayer. Often, their meetings would begin and end with the Lord's Prayer. In the arguments that went on in these councils, Jesus words of "Forgive us our trespasses," was sorely needed!

An offering of sidebars might be of interest to you:

- The title 'Christian' was not used until the second generation of Jewish and Gentile followers. Translating the Hebrew and Aramaic term 'Messiah' into Greek, the word becomes 'Christian.'
- It took 400 years for Christianity to become an accepted worldwide Faith. Constantine the Great ordered that the new religion, Christianity, become the state religion for all of the Roman Empire.
- A most important book was written by two ladies, Rita Nakashima Brock and Rebecca Ann Parker, titled *Saving Paradise – How Christianity Traded Love of This World for Crucifixion and Empire*. The details are overwhelming; however, they do explain how our religion, the manner in which we express our Faith, went from the identification of the fish to that of the cross. Their first sentence in the prologue reads, "It took Jesus a thousand years to die. Images of his corpse did not appear in churches until the tenth century." Consider how, for ten centuries, Jesus was worshipped and glorified as The One who walked among us, teaching The Way. The concentration was on life—and living rightly to the fullest. Take this lesson from their book: Cry only on Good Friday. His death was painfully cruel and awful. The rest of your days: Live with Joy.

The Historical Significance
of the Lord's Prayer
Introduction to The World's Greatest Prayer

Jesus loved to pray day or night, surrounded by people or alone, in the middle of giving a lesson, or when an answer to a question was required. His Disciples, Followers, and groups of people from all over Palestine, and visitors from foreign lands, found Jesus's prayer life a source of amazement. This incredulity took the form of wonderment, bewilderment, fascination, and an effort worthy of study. No one in Palestine prayed like this Prophet or Healer or whatever one proclaimed Him to be. Even His Apostles could only stand in wonderment of the draw 'prayer' had over their Master.

After months of watching Jesus at prayer, the Apostles finally approached Him with a request. *"Lord, teach us to pray, just as John taught his disciples,"* (Luke 11:1). John the Baptist was not only Jesus's cousin, as his mother and Jesus's mother were relatives (Luke 1:36). John was also Jesus's forerunner, announcing His coming, *"I am the voice of one crying out in the wilderness, 'Make straight the way of the Lord,'"* (John 1:23), repeating the words of Prophet Isaiah. No prayers are recorded as being either said by the Baptist or any taught to his disciples. However, their ministries were quite similar, for the Baptists preached repentance, and baptism. In a timely manner, he encouraged personal preparation for the coming Messiah.

Another similarity between Jesus and John the Baptist was their reliance on prayer. John's words were often reminiscent of Prophet Isaiah's, so it is safe to assume that the Baptist taught his disciples to 'talk' with God, just like Prophet Isaiah talked with and about God (see the OT book, Isaiah). Both the Baptist and Jesus often spoke on the

Kingdom, and it is certainly possible that, as mentioned by *christianity.stackexchange.com*, "If Jesus taught 'May your Kingdom come', then John might have taught 'Prepare us for your coming kingdom' or something like that." The freedom to speak openly and honestly with Mighty God, Creator of All, instead of just mimicking words, must have been both exciting and frightening.

Jesus knew it would be difficult to stop the ingrained habit of repeating prayers, word for word. They had been memorized since childhood and said daily from memory. One did not even have to think.

That was the problem. Memorization does not come from the heart. So when the Apostles made this request of Jesus, like the rabbi He was, Jesus taught them the simplest of prayers, words that could easily be remembered. So how is this any different from what they had been taught? The difference is, after every single phrase, there is room and purpose—in pausing! Here, one stops and thinks, and feels, and shares. Here, one speaks to Abba, our Father, personally, openly, honestly. Here, one can add their own words.

Direct contact with our Father was, and is, essential. The Apostles immediately recognized this fact. As Jesus spoke more of the bleak coming days, the possibility of His death (trying to prepare them for the worst), the more urgent it became for the Apostles to teach Jesus's Prayer to the groups that crowded daily around them. Jesus first offered the prayer to the Apostles and then to the masses who listened to His sermons from the Mount. There was time for the prayer to spread around the land prior to Pentecost. After Jesus's death, the Lord's Prayer became paramount to anyone who says, "*Messiah, I believe.*"

To be able to repeat the very words that Jesus spoke is a powerful feeling. The first Believers must have felt privileged to utter the words. Their pauses must have vibrated with thoughts and feelings, anticipation, and happiness. Meeting in private homes (mentioned throughout Acts and other NT books), the small groups of Believers became like family members. As we say today, 'they had one another's backs' in their world of suspicion and hostility. The Lord's Prayer offered them a bonding experience as they prayed in the likeness of mind. They could join hands, exchange smiles, and connect as a group with the Holy Spirit as our Lord and Father looked on. As the prayer ended, the prayerers would experience—what Jesus did so many times—joy, rejuvenation of mind and body, and clarity of purpose after having spoken with Father in this most extraordinary two-way means of open communication.

This feeling of privilege would have continued throughout the centuries of the Primitive Church (from 70 C.E. to the fourth century). Only after Constantine the Great was the church developed enough to bring forth its liturgical formats and languages, edicts, doctrines, etc., that taught what and how to believe.

One piece of liturgy within the Primitive Church was not changed, and that is The Lord's Prayer. It stands on its tradition and its merit. Language translations have not altered or harmed the integrity of our Lord's words. We can thank the writings of the Gospels for this gift of permanency, for Matthew and Luke recorded its terms for all perpetuity. The prayer appeared in the allimportant book, *The Teaching of the Twelve Apostles*, better known to us as the *Didache*, the first Christian teaching book for the laity.

It did not matter if the prayerers spoke in Aramaic, Hebrew, or Greek. Soon, the prayer would be uttered in Latin, in English, and the Scottish and Irish brogues as missionaries began to travel into known and unknown lands. One of Jesus's most important legacy to us was to teach us how to talk to Father with a prayer on our lips!

Where to Find the Lord's Prayer Phrases

ALL phrases in the Lord's Prayer are in the Old Testament. Essential religious thoughts and important spiritual themes vibrate throughout time, knowing no bounds, continuing their gathering, and growing sphere. There is nothing new under the sun (Ecclesiastes 1:9). What is new is the way we think about concepts. This unique manner of thinking creates the possibility of changing rituals within religious rites. Consider the sacrifice of animals for the forgiveness of sins. The manners in which belief systems form, and are forced to change from within or without, are all part and parcel of human advancement in spiritual journeys that have the potential to bring us ever closer to the apex of our humanity. This statement is the same truism today as it was in yesteryears.

The Lord's Prayer in the Hebrew Testaments and in the Old Testament English Translations

The first conversion given is from *The Jewish Study Bible* which contains the Tanakh translation of the Torah, Nevi'im, and Kethuvim. Immediately below that verse, find its counterpart in one of the following readings: (1) an *Authorized King James Version of Old Testament*, as this version is closer to the Greek and Latin original language translations, and (2) the *Ryrie Study Bible*. (3) Apocrypha verses contain a few verses from the Tanakh (the Jewish Holy Bible) that also contain prayer phrases. They come from the book, *The New Oxford Annotated Bible with the Apocrypha*.

The following verses are presented to you, underlined in the order of our Lord's Prayer:

"OUR FATHER"

- "Surely You are <u>our Father</u>: Though Abraham regard us not, And Israel recognize us not, You, O Lord, are <u>our Father</u>." Isaiah 63:16 [Nevi'im]
- "Doubtless thou art <u>our father</u>, though Abraham be ignorant of us, and Israel acknowledge us not: thou, O Lord, art <u>our father</u>, our redeemer; thy name is everlasting." Isaiah 63:16 [KJV]

"WHO ART IN HEAVEN"

- "To <u>You, enthroned in heaven,</u> I turn my eyes." Psalm 123:1 [Kethuvim]
- "To You I lift up my eyes, O <u>You who are enthroned in the heavens</u>!" Psalm 123:1 [Ryrie]

"HALLOWED BE THY NAME"

- "You shall not profane <u>My holy name,</u> that I may be sanctified in the midst of the Israelite people—I the Lord who sanctify you." Leviticus 22:32 [Torah]
- "Neither shall ye profane <u>my holy name</u>; but I <u>will be hallowed</u> among the children of Israel: I am the Lord which hallow you." Leviticus 22:32 [KJV]

"THY KINGDOM COME"

- "How great are His signs; how mighty His wonders! <u>His kingdom</u> is an <u>everlasting</u> kingdom, and His dominion endures throughout the generations." Daniel 3:33 [Kethuvim]
- "Dominion, glory, and kingship were given to him; All peoples and nations of every language must serve him. His <u>dominion is an everlasting dominion</u> that shall not pass away." Daniel 7:14 [Kethuvim]
- "How great are his are his signs! And how mighty are his wonders! His <u>kingdom is an everlasting kingdom,</u> and his dominion is from generation to generation." Daniel 4:3 [KVJ]
- "Thy kingdom is <u>an everlasting kingdom,</u> and thy dominion endureth throughout all generations." Psalm 145:13 [KJV]

"THY WILL BE DONE"

- "He spoke, and it was; He commanded, and it endured." Psalm 33:9 [Kethuvim]
- "For he spake, and it was done; he commanded, and it stood fast," (a paraphrase for 'Thy will be done'). Psalm 33:9 [KJV]
- "Teach me to do thy will; for thou art my God: thy spirit is good; lead me into the land of uprightness." Psalm 143:10 [KJV]
- "But as his will in heaven may be, so he will do." 1Maccabees 3:60 [NRSV with Apocrypha]

"ON EARTH AS IT IS IN HEAVEN"

- "Whatever the Lord desires He does in heaven and earth, in the seas and all the depths." Psalm 135:6 [Kethuvim]
- "Whatsoever the Lord pleased, that did he in heaven, and in earth, in the seas, and all deep places." Psalm 135:6 [KJV]

"GIVE US THIS DAY"

- "This is the day that the Lord has made—let us exult and rejoice on it." Psalm 118:24 [Kethuvim]
- "This is the day which the Lord hath made; we will rejoice and be glad in it." Psalm 118:24 [KJV]

"OUR DAILY BREAD"

- "You gave them bread from heaven when they were hungry, and produced water from a rock when they were thirsty." Nehemiah 9:15a [Kethuvim]
- "And gavest them bread from heaven for their hunger…" Nehemiah 9:15a [KJV]

- "The people asked, and he brought quails, and satisfied them with the <u>bread of heaven</u>." Psalm 105:40 [KJV]

"AND FORGIVE US OUR TRESPASSES"

- "Look at my affliction and suffering, <u>and forgive all my sins.</u>" Psalm 25:18 [Kethuvim]
- "Look upon mine affliction and my pain<u>; and forgive all my sins.</u>" Psalm 25:18 [KJV]

"AS WE FORGIVE THOSE THAT TRESPASS AGAINST US"

- "<u>Forgive your neighbor</u> a wrong, and then, <u>when you petition, your sins will be pardoned.</u>" Sirach 28:2 [KJV]
- "<u>Forgive your neighbor</u> the wrong he has done, and then <u>your sins will be pardoned</u> when you pray." Sirach 28:2 [NRSV with Apocrypha]

'LEAD US NOT INTO TEMPTATION'

- "The great <u>temptations</u> which thine eyes saw, and the signs, and the wonders, and the mighty hand, and the stretched out arm, whereby the Lord thy God <u>brought thee out</u>; so shall the Lord thy God do unto all the people of whom thou art afraid." Deuteronomy 7:19 [KJV]
- Note: In the Torah, Deuteronomy 7:19, there is no mention of 'temptations'; instead, the verse is a continuation of verse 18, and verse 19 begins with, "The wondrous acts that you saw…" Another book, The Five Books of Moses, has translated this verse to read, "the great trials that your eyes saw, the signs and the portents, the strong hand and the outstretched arm, by which YHWH your God took you out—thus will YHWH your God do to all the peoples of whom you are afraid."

- "Deliver me from all my transgressions (evil)." Psalm 39:8 [Kethuvim]
- "My times are in thy hand: deliver me from the hand of mine enemies, and from them that persecute me." Psalm 31:15 [KJV]

Among Early Jewish Prayers

In Jewish liturgy, a benediction is any prayer that begins or ends with the phrase, 'You are praised, O Lord' or 'Blessed art thou, O Lord.' When reading about the *Shemone Esreh* or the 18 Benedictions of the Tefillah, and in the chapter on Daily First-Century Prayers, we learned that each segment is called a *beracha*, the Hebrew word for 'benediction.' Plural segments are called *berachoth*. Within these segments, we will find terms and phrases like those used in Jesus's prayer, proving that humanity's needs are universal.

Prayerers had a choice which of the eighteen *beracha* they would pray. Time of year, season, and hour of the day, what demands there were upon the prayerer, all took part in their decision.

Refer to the pages containing the Benedictions. You will note immediately that beginning with *beracha* number four, the term 'us' appears, followed by 'we,' and then 'our.' The Lord's Prayer does not mention the prayerer with his or her petition until the fourth, fifth, and sixth stanzas.

Beracha number six states, 'Forgive us, our Father, for we have sinned against thee,' which is perfect reading as it speaks to sin being against God first, ourselves second. Unfortunately, it ends there, not mentioning, as the Lord's Prayer does, the sin committed against our neighbor.

Beracha number nine does not state 'daily bread,' but it does say, 'Bless this year.'

Jesus would have prayed all eighteen *berachoth* or portions of the prayer as often as possible. However, we do know that His life was overly crowded with activities. We also know that Jesus's communication with Father was a two-way street where He talked, and then He listened for the Will of Father. Recitation of a lengthy prayer with pauses for petitions and questions would add a considerable amount of time. Yet, Jesus would have continued to say the required number of Jewish prayers daily, as He was always faithful to the Law of Moses. When pressed for time, Jesus would have prayed the shorter acceptable version three times daily. This version included the topics of 'reward for those who do God's will, mercy for the righteous, grant us knowledge, accept our repentance, and forgive us.' Before ending His prayer, Jesus would take a moment to offer thanksgiving for His ministry's many blessings.

In the Primitive Church, it was a requirement for Christians to say the Lord's Prayer three times a day, just like with the Jewish people. Another similarity was that the *Shemone Esreh* and the Lord's Prayer was the chief prayer for both religions. Two other similarities are that both prayers could be communal or private, with petitions offered.

Likewise, from the chapter on Daily First-Century Prayers, we read about the Kaddish prayer. I have not been able to trace the source of what might be the oldest known copy of the prayer. It reads: "Exalter and hallowed by His great Name in the world which He created according to His will. May He establish His kingdom in your lifetime and in your days, and in the lifetime of the whole household of Israel, speedily and at a near time. May His great Name be praised forever and until all eternity." You will note that the prayer is extremely present-centered, with no regard for the past or future. It is a prayer that petitions the coming of the Kingdom now. The expectation for the Jewish Messiah was that He would help bring the Kingdom now, and when our Lord ascended without the presence of Heaven on Earth, no Kingdom now, those who had felt an attraction to, and even a belief in Jesus, turned their backs on Him and His teachings.

The Kaddish is an Aramaic prayer, a mourner's prayer. Its term means 'sanctification' and is akin to the Hebrew word *kadosh*, meaning 'holy.' Jesus would have been familiar with this prayer, as death was a constant in first-century Palestine. In scrutinizing the prayer, we note similar terms in the Kaddish prayer and Jesus's prayer. Both speak to God's name be hallowed, the will of God, and His kingdom come. Repeating these themes three times daily would make their importance paramount.

'God's Will' Phrase Found Among Monotheistic Religions

All new religions are influenced by older belief systems, especially since they carry the seeds the humans need to believe in something greater than themselves. We crave knowing there is a purpose to our lives, that how we live, why we live matters. The Christian religion was, in the beginning, greatly influenced by the Jewish religion. Later, according to *The Great Religions* by J. F. Clarke, the belief systems of Egypt, Greece, and Rome influenced Christianity. In turn, sacred writings from Persia, Babylon, and Egypt influenced the Jewish religion.

We reviewed how concepts in the Lord's Prayer were already themes in Jewish prayers. The same is true about verses in the Persian Zendavesta. The Zend-Avesta is the Bible and the Prayer Book of Zoroaster, written in the Middle Persian language, centuries before the Christian period. In similarity to the Jewish and Christian religions, according to *en.wikisource.org*, this religion contains concepts of *Yashts* (angels) who serve as messengers for God while contending with the destructive forces of demons, whose leader is the Devil. Their books tell the tales of men whose legends of heroic deeds match those of the Old Testament. One part of the Persian Zendavesta is *Yasna*, its chief liturgical recitation consisting mainly of praise and thanksgiving. J. F. Clarke notes that the all-encompassing sphere of this belief system is the

Kingdom of God whose divine will guides the peace-loving people who worship under this banner. It is a small religion that is still in existence today.

Around 1,000 B.C.E., Hinduisms' four Vedas (books of knowledge) offer us a Heaven-Father and an Earth Mother. *The World's Living Religions* offer glimpses into its psalms, filled with the omnipresence and omniscience of heaven, and its prayers, such as 'Heaven is my Father, Progenitor! There is my origin' (Rig Veda, 1:164.33). The book offers us a look into their belief system of a Creator God who wants worshippers to seek His will, 'And may He direct our thoughts!' (Rig Veda, 3:62.10).

Briefly, these three great monotheistic religions of Islam, Judaism, and Christianity have this to say about the Will of God:

- Mohammed (or Muhammad) instructed his followers: "When you pray to God, do not say, 'If it be Thy Will…' but be in importunate and demand great things, for nothing is difficult for God."
- Judaism's belief system regarding the will of God is found in 1Maccabees 3:60, "But as his will in heaven may be, so he will do."
- Christianity's belief system concerning the will of God is found in Matthew 6:10b, "Thy will be done on earth as it is in heaven."

There are people saddened by the thought that Christianity is not unique in concepts, themes, or philosophies. Your author wishes we could all take comfort in knowing that our One God existed before time and will continue to be beyond eternity. Ecclesiastes 1:9 writes, "There is nothing new under the sun," which is the good news. This is a statement of comfort, as it brings forth the knowledge that humanity continues its divine quest of independent yet together, spiritual journeys. We gain, we fall back, sometimes one step forward with two steps back, but we are resilient, pick up the pieces, and move forward. Humans are 'hope-ers'—always hoping that whatever the problem is, change is forthcoming. As we falter, we stop yet again to explore possibilities, to seek the Will of God. On the right steppingstone, the right path, our journey moves forward. Off the path, a misstep, little is right in our lives. Our earthly job is to mature spiritually. We do this by appreciating and caring for the blessings of our life: the earth, our relationships, our given talents, and our steadfastness in our Faith. Prayer and prayer answers guide us. Seeking the Will of our Creator puts us in touch with the struggles encountered in the long past of our progenitors and places us somewhere in the middle of a long future for humanity. The higher we reach for the apex of our humanness, the more advanced our descendants will be.

Love, Forgiveness, and Making It Right with One's Neighbor

Often, too often, following the Will of God leads us to the path of most resistance. Jesus wisely included in His prayer: "Forgive us our trespasses as we forgive those who trespass against us." Wow, wait! I want forgiveness for my sins. I do not want to forgive that 'other' who wronged me! I want him/her punished. I seek—well, not annihilation. That is a bit strong. How about 'reprisal'? A little tiny bit? No. Cannot have it. Feel bad for thinking it, much less desiring it.

Two little letters, 'a' and 's', simply cannot be this important! Yet, according to our loving Lord, who wants us to live into the goodness and purity of our Faith, we ought not to seek forgiveness for ourselves until we have first given—carte blanche—forgiveness to the 'other(s).' Period.

King David's knowledge about forgiveness came to him the hard way! After all, Saul was treacherous, and even tried to kill him. His lust for Bathsheba, and his murder of her husband, Joab, was an awful two-strike sin. Yet, God did not leave David alone to deal with this issue as an advisor was sent to him.

Gad the Prophet was the king's friend and spiritual counselor. In his writing, *The Testament of Gad*, the prophet penned a prayer on forgiveness: "Love ye one another from the heart; and if a man sin against thee, speak peaceably to him…and he if repent and confess, forgive him… But if he be shameless and persisteth in his wrongdoing, even so, forgive him." Jesus brought this a step forward by saying, "Turn the other cheek." And we can believe that Gad the Prophet shared this philosophy with King David!

The Holy Bible often speaks of the terrible price paid for wrongdoing. Second Samuel 12:1–23 relates how Bathsheba and King David's firstborn son died after being ill for seven days because of their sins and the lack of seeking forgiveness for the murder of her husband. A child dying for the sins of the parents is an uncomfortable thought. However, this type of statement goes along with the 'eye for an eye' punishment theology, as well as the ritual sacrifice.

Jesus's theology has nothing to do with this reasoning. And maybe, just maybe, this is why our Lord used the term 'as'—to reinforce its necessity. Why should we forgive?

Reason one, so that the actions of others do not diminish the love in our hearts.

Reason two, so that we remain in healthy relationship with our neighbor.

Reason three, so that we remain steadfast in our commitment to continue in our spiritual journey.

No one needs a stumbling block—which lack of forgiveness is—in our minds, hearts, and spiritual lives. It comes down to asking the question, "What is most important to me?" If your answer does not include living right with your Maker, then reading books like this one will not help resolve the problems in your life.

The Lord's Prayer is our banner under which we march. The prayer keeps us on the 'striving for holiness' track. Leaders in the Jewish and Christian religions have long recognized the help and the importance of forgiveness as Jesus spoke it. Shortly after the death of Jesus, a rabbi wrote in Yoma 8:9, "Transgressions between a man and his neighbor are not expiated by the Day of Atonement unless the man first makes peace with his neighbor." In 96 C.E. in First Clement 13:2, Clement of Rome wrote, "Be merciful, and you will find mercy; forgive, and you will be forgiven." In the third century C.E., Rabbi Yannai developed this petition: "Lead me not into the power of sin, not into the power of transgression and not into the power of temptation and not into the power of shame." The term 'power' is entirely appropriate when dealing with the issue of forgiveness.

The significance and value of the issue of forgiveness continue to this day. Our innate desire is to be right with our Father, right with ourselves, and with one another. We painfully discover that not being right with any one of these means we are not right with all of them. And so, the struggle continues. Thankfully, our Lord gave us His prayer to help us along the way.

The Three Gospels Come to Life

IMPORTANT NOTE TO READERS: The chapters that follow will all contain information that derived, over a three-decade period, from the list of books, Holy Bibles, and research, most of them listed in this book's nine-page bibliography section. These books, in some manner, shared the information presented here. Your benefit is in not having to read through the 90-some books to ascertain the data! People who write about our Lord's Prayer share information and thoughts. Thousands upon thousands of books exists on this topic. It is doubtful that deciphering the originator of a fact, written statement, or impression is possible. We each share in the glory of our Faith.

Below is your author's original drawing of what began as the three-part usually seen *Quelle* (a German word, *Quellen*, means 'to well up,' and this came to mean *Quella*, 'spring' and *Quelle*, 'source') depiction of the Synoptic Gospels. In Greek, the term synoptic means 'a seeing together,' and because Matthew and Luke together contain information found in Mark—written first—the three Gospels are grouped as the 'Synoptic Gospels.'

The chart you are looking at is a representation of how Mark, Matthew, and Luke came together. The chart's solid lines represent the three Gospels, with Mark, the originator, on top, and Matthew and Luke spreading out below. The traditions from Antioch, the Infancy Narrative sources, and the proto-Luke 700 verses, and, later, the Mark, Luke, and Q verses became additions to the chart.

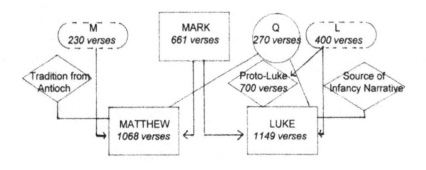

The Q source may have had 270 verses that contributed to Matthew and Luke's stories. However, there is no existing copy of Q. It is undoubtedly one of the oldest sources, dating from the time of Jesus to around 50 C.E. Losing the entire copy of Q was a terrible loss, as we believe Q included oral statements from the Apostles, and actual eyewitnesses to Jesus's teachings, healings, and Jesus-events. The words of persons who personally knew Jesus, and some who had the closest of ties with Jesus, are lost forever to us. The Q Source is considered the most reliable oral tradition we could have had concerning our Lord. Its original recorded writings would have been priceless for the information it encompassed.

You will note that Q verses contributed to the work of Matthew and Luke but not Mark. This might account for some of the stories found in those Gospels but not in Mark. Independent versus individually found in each of the three might pertain to their communities' concerns. They might also have come to the writers from an oral source or a few written sources. There is no way of knowing for sure.

Writing of the Gospels' Prayer

Initially, all four Gospels were written in Greek, and they were written either by one individual or by a group, sometimes classified as a 'school.' The writers lived, taught, and led churches in Greece, Rome, Asia Minor, and Syria. On their own, having only their personal experiences and limited missionary training, these leaders of widely separated churches were not of the same opinion in such important topics as Christian membership, doctrine, or theology. Their diversity caused multiple problems when it came time for the Christian religion to be gathered under the single roof of the Church of Rome.

The four Gospels appeared between 50 and 100 C.E. The Gospel According to Mark was written first, between the mid-to-late 50s by Mark. His name also appears in Acts 12.12, 25; 15.37–39 as John Mark. For this writing, we will call him "Mark". In Acts 12:25 and 15:36–40, Mark is the companion of Paul and Barnabus. More importantly, Apostle Peter gave him reports of the words and deeds of Jesus, as did Apostle John, who later wrote the Gospel of John while in exile. Probably, Mark took Peter's report while Peter was publicly preaching in Rome. By this late date, Apostle Peter would be reconciled to the fact that Jesus would be the founder of a new religion known as Christianity and not the Messiah of the Jews as Apostle Peter originally believed Him to be. Whether or not Apostle Peter encouraged Mark to write for the Gentiles is unknown. What is known is that Mark intended his writings for the Gentile Christian communities.

The Gospel According to Mark stands out on three points:

1. Wanting Gentiles to understand, John Mark describes the unfamiliar Jewish ceremonial rites and customs when Jesus referred to them, sometimes in a disapproving or negative manner.
2. Roman and Jewish law differed on most points, and John Mark explained those differences to exhibit the stress and tensions between the two nations.
3. Aramaic phrases will not be found in Mark's Gospel, as he translated all of them for the Gentile readers and listeners.

Your author has not found anyone offering a reasonable answer as to why Mark did not include the Lord's Prayer in his Gospel, especially since believers already spoke the prayer in Rome.

The Gospel According to Matthew was written in fluent Greek between the late 50s to early 60s. Long ago, it was believed a converted rabbi wrote the Gospel of Matthew because:

1. The Gospel's take on Jewish matters is quite apparent.
2. Ample proof shows how Jesus fulfilled Old Testament prophecies.
3. Jesus' attitude toward Jewish Law is stressed.
4. To reinforce the belief of a rabbi authorship, it was thought that the Gospel was written in Antioch of Syria for a large Jewish Christian community.

Apostle Matthew wrote his Gospel, using his name and personal experience with our Lord. His writing is brutally honest, giving no quarter to either himself or Jesus. He is the one who pointed out that he was a betrayer of his people by collecting Roman taxes from them. When Jesus flew into a rage in the Temple, Matthew wrote of it.

Apostle Matthew emphasized in his writing:

1. The Kingdom.
2. The fulfilment of Jewish prophecies in Jesus.
3. The eschatology doctrine of 'last things' – second coming, end of the age, the final Judgment.
4. The continuation of Jesus's ministry. He was the only Apostle to use the term 'church'—wherein a gathering of our Lord's people would congregate.

The Gospel According to Luke is unique. Even though it shares with Matthew bits and pieces of Mark's Gospel, it is a Book One of a set. It could have been titled, 'The Life of Jesus,' and Book Two could have been titled, 'Acts: The Growth of the Christian Church.' Luke was a native Syrian, born in Antioch, a trained physician, and a second-generation member of the Early Church. Luke's Gospel and Acts were written in Achaia, around 64 C.E. Acts underwent a revision in the 80s. Luke became Paul's legal expert and traveled extensively as his companion. For this reason, Luke's Gospel received what the Church of Rome calls 'apostolic endorsement' by virtue of Paul's authority.

The Authorities Agree

Theologians and scholars work hard to bring understanding into the complicated matters of our Faith. Primarily, two processes help bring a flow of steppingstones of clarity rather than conclusions.

The first process is called 'Redaction Criticism,' which merely means being critical of the writer's editorial decisions. This examination attempts to understand how and why each writer selected and edited the information collected, whether it be of the oral or written traditions. One note of puzzling interest is how, in using the method of redaction criticism, the examiners agreed that Matthew and Luke Lord's prayers could not have come from the Q source because of the amount of variation between them.

The second process at obtaining the 'truth' is done through a 'Criterion of Distinctiveness,' meaning that interpreters of the Gospels attempt to identify what are the authentic teachings and sayings of Jesus. In other words, the phrases and statements attributed to Jesus cannot have any relationship to any of the ideas or parallels to Judaism, the Primitive Church (40 to 70 C.E.), or to the Early Church (after 70 C.E.).

When combining these two processes, authorities agree that the Lord's Prayer is authentically Jesus's work. Here are four primary reasons:

1. Using the term 'Abba' for God, as "our" Father, is an intimate and familiar Aramaic address. While Jewish families spoke this

word within the family unit, it was unusual to hear it referring to God, Creator of the Universe.

2. Jesus introduced new concepts into what the Kingdom of God embodied.

3. Jesus proclaimed that to receive our Father's forgiveness we first have to offer our forgiveness to those who trespassed against us.

4. Jesus's name does not appear in the prayer, nor is there any reference to Him. Based upon these points, this proved to the examiners that the Primitive Church did not have a hand in creating this prayer, as they believed the Primitive Church would have added Jesus's name.

In the next chapters, we will discover differences between the Lord's Prayer in Matthew and Luke Gospels. While we have not examined any other works, note that other disparities in the Gospels exists, such as between the writings of the Beatitudes and the Golden Rule. The timing of events, along with the settings, also show differences.

Readers of the Gospels should anticipate differences in that they were penned by persons with their mindsets and problems, writing in different lands, years apart, and depending upon various resources. Omissions may or may not have been done purposefully. It could merely have been a matter of not being privy to the information.

The bottom line is that we have the choice of nitpicking and finding fault. Or, we can say, "Thank you, Lord. What a lot of food for thought!"

Matthew's Unique Lord's Prayer with Nine Points Emphasized

Matthews's Gospel offers the Lord's Prayer for the first time during Jesus's teachings on the Sermon on the Mount. The sermon began as a broad set of verbal lessons given by Jesus to His Disciples. Given this fact, it should not be a surprise that those many teachings would have taken a minimum of three days to deliver. The lessons encapsulate what will be most of Jesus's education over the next three years. They would make a great, if overwhelming, source of information to be discussed and analyzed for years to come.

Instead, we learn that vast crowds of people followed Jesus to the Mount (Mt. 7.28–8.1), prepared to stay with Him, though there is no mention of food, drink, or bedding for the men, women, and children in the crowd. Another element of surprise is that Matthew offers this extraordinary, extensive range of topics covering morality, ethics versus law, to human behaviors, criminal actions, and community responsibilities.

Your author strongly questions the placement of the sermon early on in Matthew mainly because the rest of the Gospels speak to how, at the onset, Jesus's Listeners and Followers were few in numbers. Teachings were not what they wanted. What drew crowds to Jesus were His healings. He was not like the other Prophet-Healers that traversed the Palestinian land. He was not called a magician for long because His cures of the mentally ill (demon-filled), the lepers, the blind, and the dying were real. And there were far too many for anyone to yell, "Fake!" The Gospels relate that Jesus taught while healing. What he taught is among the teachings on the Mount. But to say that the Mount experience occurred so shortly after is a misnomer because: one, being baptized by John; two, spending 40 days and 40 nights undergoing temptations; and three, journeying through Zebulun, Naphtali, and Galilee, while teaching and healing, is a bit of a stretch. Common sense tells us it took time for the populace to learn about Jesus, His healings and teachings. What is important is that, at a point in His ministry, Jesus heads for the nearest mountain and begins to teach to large crowds His life's lessons and offerings from a Mount (Mt. 3.13–5.1a).

One offering from the Mount was the Lord's Prayer [Mt. 5:614]. Before giving the prayer, Jesus speaks about almsgiving. Then He offers His prayer, followed by instructions on fasting. It is not difficult for us to make a correlation between the topics for almsgiving opens the heart, Jesus's prayer opens the soul, and fasting opens the mind.

The Matthewian Version of the Lord's Prayer

'Our Father in heaven,
hallowed be your name.
Your kingdom come,
your will be done,
on earth as it is in heaven.
Give us this day our daily bread,
and forgive us our debts,
as we also have forgiven our debtors.
And lead us not into temptation,
but deliver us from evil.'
Matthew 6:9–13 English Standard Version [ESV]

The nine comparison points often emphasized in writings about the Lord's Prayer include:

1. The Matthew version contains characteristics of Jewish prayer.
2. 'My Father' opens many Jewish prayers, and Jesus's prayer is 'our Father.'
3. God is addressed as the second person in the Jesus's prayer.
4. Jesus's prayer is of a simplistic style, while Jewish prayer is often multi-layered
5. Jewish prayer can be lengthy, whereas the Lord's Prayer is short.
6. Liturgical benedictions, otherwise known as 'priestly blessings,' are often a requirement in offering prayer. The Lord's Prayer does not require priestly blessing
7. s, making it perfect for a private petition.
8. "The Kingdom come" is a common theme in both Jewish and Christian prayer. The difference is the degree of emphasis given to the word 'come.' In Jewish prayer, there is sometimes urgency to the term, whereas in Christian prayer, there appears to be an understanding that there is work for Christians to accomplish before the kingdom arrives on Earth.

9. When comparing the Luke and Matthew prayer differences, we discover that the Matthewian Prayer becomes more popular with the Galilean church, whose churches had formed an authoritative base. Jerusalem finally took this position, and they adopted the Matthewian Prayer in toto, not making a single change.

10. Another argument favoring the Matthewian Prayer over the Lucian Lord's Prayer is the rhythm of its words and sentence structures. It has good flow while being pleasing to the ear and the tongue. These attributes have made it popular for private prayer and church liturgies.

Luke's Unique Lord's Prayer with Ten Points Emphasized

Early in Luke, the Pharisees and Teachers of the Law were quite angry with Jesus's behavior. Our Lord was supposed to be representing a holy man's behavior, given to ethical teachings, and mild-mannered speech. Instead, Jesus stood accused of being a drunkard and a glutton (Mt. 11:19). Now, this comparison is being given to Jesus's' men, for, in Luke 5:33, the group says, "John's disciples often fast and pray, and so do the disciples of the Pharisees, but yours go on eating and drinking." This passage shows that John the Baptist's disciples were widely known to be prayerers.

Since Jesus was also well-known to be a great prayerer, His Apostles desired to emulate their master. They were unsure how best to offer an intimate petitionary prayer to Father since this was not according to their custom.

Jesus delivered Matthew's prayer in the Galilean territory. Luke's request for this teaching probably occurred one year later, while the group traveled in Perea, in the Jordan Valley. The Jordan River flowed nearby, thus reminding the traveling group of their baptisms.

The difference in the territory is also a reminder to readers that the Lord's Prayer, written in Luke's Gospel, is less Hebrew in format and contains more Gentile terms. The intended audience is always an important consideration when studying the Holy Bible's writings.

The Lucian Version of the Lord's Prayer
"Father, hallowed by your name.
Your kingdom come.
Give us each day our daily bread,
And forgive us our sins,
For we ourselves forgive everyone who is indebted to us.
And lead us not into temptation."
Luke 11:2b–4, New American Standard Bible [NASB]

In Luke's treatment, Jesus gave the Apostles their prayer with the following differences:

1. Matthew's prayer was given at the beginning of Jesus's ministry (6:9–13), while Luke's prayer was given halfway through his Gospel (11:2–4).
2. Fewer disciples heard the prayer early in the Mount sermon, as the entire twelve Apostles had yet to be chosen by Jesus.
3. The prayer was offered to Jesus's many listeners in Matthew but only privately to His Apostles in Luke. It was the custom of the time that rabbis offered their disciples a prayer especially created for them.
4. The Matthew prayer is more extended than Luke's prayer while still covering the same main points.
5. Since Jesus did pray often, He may have wanted to give to His Apostles a prayer they could say in short moments of silence, or maybe when a special petition was needed.
6. The Apostles would certainly have been very aware of how Jesus often returned from His time spent praying, appearing rejuvenated and at peace. Surely, they sought these feelings for

themselves and would eagerly engage themselves in Jesus's offering.

7. At this point in their ministerial training, the Apostles would be mature enough to realize that this offering was short and to the point so that their petitions could flow with the same pointed shortness.

8. The Apostles could take this new version of the Lord's Prayer out into the populace where their Gentile listeners would gladly receive the prayer for its brevity and pleasing terms. Gentiles were more used to praying to household and multiple temple gods. News of the one God, along with a prayer to 'our Father,' would have, indeed, been glad tidings.

9. Many scholars believe that the Lucian form is the prayer Jesus favors for use by prayerers. Jesus's criticism of the Pharisee's manner of lengthy, showy prayers goes against His teaching that brevity in prayer is preferred. The offering of this Lucian prayer certainly fulfils His preference.

10. There is a shared belief that Luke's prayer is too short to be used for liturgical use.

Unshared Matthew and Luke Phrases

Minutia is alive and well when it comes to examining terms and phrases utilized in the Holy Bible. Jesus's prayer has undergone scrutinization to the fullest. Below are four such examples:

- Maybe because Aramaic is a dead written language, the difficulty translators had with the Aramaic writing is why the two prayers are different.

- Matthew wrote, 'Thy will be done on earth as it is in heaven,' while Luke only wrote, 'Thy kingdom come.' Could Luke have felt that his statement says the same as wordy Matthew's does?

- Is not 'Thy will be done' a foregone conclusion? Why speak in prayer what is already known to be true?

One shortcut not taken was with the sentence, 'And forgive us our debts, as we also have forgiven our debtors' (Matthew), and with the sentence, 'And forgive us our sins, for we ourselves forgive everyone who is indebted to us' (Luke). The sameness here is almost startling. Could this be because of the importance Jesus places on forgiveness?

Yet, what strikes your author is the inclusion of the word 'ourselves' in the Luke version. The Roman Catholic, American Episcopal, Anglican, and Lutheran denominations, as well as the smaller denominational and community churches, use the Lord's Prayer in their liturgical worship service. The 'we forgive everyone' can become corporate, shared forgiveness. While there is certainly a place for group forgiveness toward those perpetrating harm against our air, water, animals, people of specific color or relations or nationalities, we still need—no, require—that 'we ourselves,' do become 'I' do forgive you.

Differences between Luke's and Matthew's Lord's Prayer

Depending upon one's view, either Luke or Matthew can be the 'original' prayer. Philip Hamer, in his book. Understanding the Lord's Prayer, and Andres Fernandez in his The Life of Christ book, point out the differences listed below. Other authors have also pointed out these contrasts in their writings.

Matthew: 'Our Father, who art in heaven' versus Luke: 'Father.'

Matthew: 'Thy will be done, on earth as it is in heaven' versus Luke: absent.

Matthew: 'But deliver us from evil' versus Luke: absent.

Differences where word usage and word tense are apparent:

- Matthew's use of 'debts' is a common Jewish religious term, for God was understood to be the 'Great Creditor' to whom all was due. Luke, on the other hand, uses the word 'trespasses,' which would have been understood and appreciated by the Gentiles, as 'sin' was already a long-standing part of their vocabulary.
- Matthew says, "As we have forgiven," which is a past tense statement, while Luke says, "As we also forgive," which is in the present tense, where Jesus liked to keep His teachings.
- Another more in keeping with Jesus's teachings is Luke's use of, 'Forgive us, for we also forgive,' which speaks to unconditional forgiveness. In contrast, while Matthew's statement of, 'Forgive us, as we forgive,' speaks to conditional forgiveness.
- The differences in length between the two prayers continue to bother many scholars and students of the Holy Bible. A trend now is to point to the differences in the location where the prayer was said, and how that particular church functioned.
- Matthew 6:7 quotes Jesus as saying, "And in praying, do not heap up empty phrases." Does anyone believe either or Luke would ever have added or deleted what Jesus said? So we have an oxymoron. How did the two prayers end up with such different lengths?

Lack of the Lord's Prayer in the Gospels of Mark and John

The fact that neither Mark nor John included the Lord's Prayer in the Gospels has caused speculation. Consider for a moment: does it make sense that one would consist of four repetitive stories of similar events and statements? Matthew and Luke already suffer from overlapping. Why add two more repetitious Gospels?

The Gospel According to Mark was written first and did not include the Lord's Prayer. The exclusion has caused statements by scholars saying that Jesus never said this prayer, that it was formulated by the

Primitive Church, who needed a liturgical prayer for their services. The Primitive Church could have used Jesus's own words found in the Gospel According to Mark, especially in 11:23b–26. The similarity in writing here with those used in Jesus's prayer will jump out at the reader. In chapter 14:36, Jesus prays in the Garden of Gethsemane, "Not what I will, but what You will," and, again, in 14:38, "And pray, lest you enter into temptation." (NKJV)

These are valid arguments that account for their continued existence. However, the Gospel According to John appeared last, and it does not include the Lord's Prayer. How, then, does the argument that the Primitive Church wrote this prayer account for its omission from John's Gospel?

The fact remains that the Lord's Prayer is not in either Mark's or John's Gospels. Another argument for its exclusion is that neither the baptismal rite nor meeting for religious services on Sunday receives mention in the New Testament. Could it be that all three, Jesus's prayer, baptism, and Sunday services, were part of the church's liturgical regularity? Or that what established practices there were never received inclusion because their widespread acceptance was not an issue? There is also the point that familiarity breeds a lack of attention. One might not even think about what occurs routinely.

One more omission in Apostle John's Gospel needs addressing. By the time John reached an advanced age, the thought is he might have become a mystic. His writings in the Book of Revelation certainly proves this possibility. Mystics do not believe in corporate prayer because prayer is an extraordinary, very inward outpouring. Apostle John was also an absolute firm believer in the state of pure sinlessness in Jesus. Therefore, John the Beloved would never have written, 'and forgive US our trespasses' for Jesus never spoke of Himself as having sin or being in sin.

How the Primitive and Early Churches Utilized the Lord's Prayer

Note: again, the nine pages of bibliography contain the list of books from which the following information derives.

Political and social inner strife appears to have been an almost-lifelong, ongoing condition between the Jewish citizens and their religious hierarchy. The three books of the Maccabees family and their rebelling troops occupied Palestine politics through skirmishes, politics, and battles from 168–165 B.C.E. Then, the Hasmonean Revolt took place, with that family becoming the rulers of Palestine from 167–143 B.C.E. The Sicarii bands of assassins of the Zealot sect terrorized the homeland from 70–50 B.C.E. It is almost as if the powerful can overcome the resisting and resentful citizens but never for long.

The same is true of their Faith. Outside forces like the Parthian and the Assyrian armies attempted to make changes to the Jewish religion and its people. Eventually, they failed. Rome followed on their heels and, in large part, did make an impact. History shows us that around 200 B.C.E., the Jews of the Diaspora began to abandon Aramaic in favor of Greek, and, forced Hellenization of the Jewish people began in 171 B.C.E. (Daniel 11:22).

In many ways, the attraction of Hellenization had a more considerable emotional pull over the Jewish religious and wealthy citizens than that of the conquering enemies. The influence of Hellenization altered people's thinking and lives, whether they resisted or welcomed the change. Hellenization transformed their lifestyles in dress, eating, household items (introduction of the eating fork), furniture (ushering in of the table, chairs, and lounging couches), medicines, and physicians (non-Jewish doctors). Latin words and a more sophisticated way of speaking wormed their way into their speech. A class distinction between 'the worldly' and 'the commoners' became overly apparent, and this had more to do with attitude than money. Household idols appeared in dwellings of those who had business dealings with the Romans. If all of this was not enough of a problem, even more significant changes were occurring inside the synagogues.

Two Types of Jewish Worshippers

Jewish converts to Jesus's Messiahship and non-converted Jewish worshippers continued to attend services in the same synagogues throughout Palestine. In the first century, over 400 synagogues were in existence. The shared-worship services continued right up to the Jewish Dispersion in 70 C.E. After the destruction of Jerusalem and the Temple, Romans and Gentiles from other nations made their homes in Palestine where the Jewish populace was unwelcomed. Thus, the 'dispersion' of the Jewish people took their Faith, doctrines, traditions, rites, and rituals with them into other countries.

However, from the time of the death of Jesus until the Dispersion— nearly forty years the Jewish 'Brethren' (those who had converted) and Jewish worshippers attended the same synagogues, the same morning, evening, and Sabbath services. It is probably difficult for us to understand how the two different sets of beliefs could have fared under the same roof, but they did. Your author imagines that some pretty lively discussions took place after the services!

Later, when the Roman army swept in, literally tearing pieces of the Jerusalem Temple apart with their bare hands and parading their 'trophies' of Holy Temple relics in the street, the Brethren had to make the hard decision. With no turning back possible, to be or not, give up family and friends or not, to walk away from a tribal identity. It must have been like taking one's root, the essence of being, and cutting it in half. All that was can no longer be anything more than a memory.

Decision time.

- Choice One: remaining in the Jewish Faith was to assert belief in their fathers' Hebrew Faith. Their long-awaited-for Messiah had yet to appear. Jesus from Nazareth had been a great healing, teaching rabbi. They had learned from His words, and they had had plenty of opportunities to see how far they had strayed from Moses's instructions. Another option was to show a mild interest in the events surrounding His ministry but ignore His teachings.
- Choice Two: chose a new path, the new life. Forego tradition, family, community. Begin anew by following the steppingstones of Messiah Jesus, joining Him in a world where the possibility of Heaven is right here on Earth. As a Brethren, have a hand in bringing this closeness about. Be a part of the exciting new order of enduring Faith. Engage in the holy fellowship by being a member of the Brethren.

If an individual felt 'locked' in his Jewish Faith, isolated from the world, and all the terrible happenings occurring in and around it, the New Life religion had to look enticing. Free from the restraints of 613 religious laws, the "outside world" had an appeal: advances in travel, housing comfort, medicine, and medical care for the ill and injured, more socially acceptable interactions between the sexes, an opportunity to explore open fields of education, especially the classes and debates on religion and philosophy, had to have had a strong pull. A door had opened, and life spoke to a freedom previously unknown to them.

Growth of the Jewish Christian (Brethren) Church

Following the four Gospels in the New Testament is The Acts of the Apostles, better known as its shorten version, 'Acts'. Within its pages, Chapters 8, 13, 14, 17–19, 22, and 23 tell of the early growth of the Christian Faith among the Jewish people who worshipped in the already existing Palestinian synagogues. They had previously established four hundred buildings making it possible for the Christian Faith to experience rapid growth.

When a person incorporates a new piece of information into their belief system (or any other kind of structure), the understanding is that an 'expansion' has taken place. The same is true with what happened next within this motherdaughter Faith. The Brethren did not see themselves as 'fallen Jews.' There was nothing 'fallen' about believing Jesus to be the Messiah or about the new joy and privilege of being in a closer, more intimate relationship with God. According to Acts 17:10, there was even one synagogue-church in Beroea where all the congregants worshipped Jesus as the Messiah.

The fact that these attitudes permeated existing synagogues caused little problem as the two opposing sides each saw one another as persons to win over to their side. A privately held belief that Jesus was the Messiah caused no alarm because, for the steadfast Jewish faithful, Jesus was a passing craze. However, when the Apostles and Disciple leaders began preaching in the synagogues in the name of Jesus Christ, their long-awaited-for Messiah, the two beliefs ceased to be one.

The Brethren saw nothing wrong with this newly introduced public statement. They were actually pleased to hear it coming from their pulpit, but the Jewish congregation was not. They liked it when the Brethren spoke on Jesus' teachings, and telling them about His healings. People in both groups hungered to hear about unconditional love, forgiveness of sin, forgiveness between people, and the topic of eternal life.

As far as the Brethren were concerned, embracing peoples of different religious beliefs, skin colors, or nationalities, was a joyous spiritual experience, for everyone was welcomed to become 'brothers and sisters' in the worldwide family of Christ-believers. The Jewish Faith had a long-established process by which one joined their Jewish religion. Not so for the Christians. A hug of 'welcome,' a baptism, and an "*I follow Jesus*" was all that was needed to become a member. It would be a longtime coming before the Church of Rome introduced catechism lessons to interested-in-the-Faith persons. Up to this point, people becoming an immediate member was more important than any 'process' for joining.

Not all synagogues were happy with the schism. There was retaliation. In the decade of 80 to 90 C.E., Samuel the Small wrote a piece at the request of Gamaliel II in Jamnia. This *beracha* became known as the Twelfth Benediction and included in the worship readings of the now 19 Benedictions. The Oxford University Press *(jstor.org)* article points to the powerful weapon this *'aposynagogoi'* verse proved to be for the Jewish community. *Aposynagogoi* is a Greek term meaning, for the Jewish community, religious separation on the one hand, and ex-communication for others.

The Benediction states:

"For the apostate let there be no hope
And let the arrogant government be speedily uprooted in our days.
Let the Nazarenes (Christians) and the Minim (heretics)
Be destroyed in a moment
And let them be blotted out of the Book of Life and
not be inscribed together with the righteous.
Blessed art Thou, O Lord, who humblest the proud!"

No Brethren could or would ascribe to verbalizing such a statement. The *beracha* must have been horrifying to them—and heartbreaking, and there would have been no choice but to leave the synagogue. However, this decision to leave the synagogue stimulated the growth of the Christian churches. Members began to meet in private homes. When the membership outgrew the room of a dwelling, and enough coin was acquired, construction on church buildings began. They were known as Hellenistic Synagogues, and the term 'synagogue' continued until the second century.

Liturgical Functions of the Lord's Prayer

Jesus never proclaimed to start a new religion. If Jesus had, we would never have heard of Him for such a proclamation would have brought an Immediate stoning death sentence by the Temple hierarchy. Instead, Jesus quietly and patiently gave us three gifts that strictly pertain to His New Life.

First, Jesus placed importance on the rite of Baptism for all adults who wanted to become a member of the family in New Life.

Second, Jesus officiated at a meal where He asked, "Do this in remembrance of me," as He and the Apostles broke bread together and took wine.

Third, we know from His many teachings that our Lord taught the simplification of Faith, and this certainly endeared Him to the people. One of His most persuasive examples of simplification involved prayer—speak to Father, no need for lengthy prayers. This teaching was repeated often in the Gospels. See Jesus's remarks about the showiness exhibited by the Pharisees (aka, 'the hypocrites') in Matthew 6:5.

The meaningfulness and popularity of the Lord's Prayer are due to five strong points:

1. Jesus, our Lord, and Savior spoke these words. In Christendom, this is probably one of the strongest beliefs when it comes to what Jesus might and might not have uttered.
2. Jesus's prayer resonates with believers because it touches the core of human needs and desires:
3. 'Our' = to be an intricate part of the human family.
4. 'Father' = to have that bond with the eternal family.
5. 'Hallowed Name' = to touch the spiritual holiness.
6. 'Your will done' = to be still, to hear, to listen, to do—all according to the Will of our Father, and for our greatest pleasure.
7. 'Kingdom come as in Heaven and on Earth = to join in Faith (our belief, ethics, behavior) can humbly help bring this about.

8. 'Daily Bread' = to have the security to live sheltered, fed, and healthy.

9. 'Forgive us as We forgive = to have the hurt, pain, disappointment of self, and others, erased from mind and heart—on Earth, in Heaven.

10. 'Temptation' = to be strong in not being led, to not succumb.

11. 'Rescue us' = to have protection from the hurts, wrongdoings, problems, and evilness perpetrated on us, and the world, by others and by circumstances.

12. The prayer's poetic rhythm is a popular topic. Pointed out are how poetry rhythms are like music, in that we are spoken to without the clutter of words, yet the rhythm can caress the soul. The prayer's phrases can roll off the tongue in a cadence that eases or strengths, depending upon need or desire. We know the pity, the shame in imploring for mercy, for forgiveness. We know gentleness. The Lord's Prayer can be our rock band who sounds the beat of emotionalism or offers a soothing lullaby of unconditional love.

13. The Lord's Prayer is universal in that almost all Christian churches utilize this prayer corporately in their Sunday services.

14. The Lord's Prayer finds its place in most liturgical offices performed by churches, such as baptism.

The Primitive Church and the early churches began to establish regularity and commonality to their services. In this regard, six offices came into existence, and each one involved the recitation of the Lord's Prayer:

One = Catechumens preparing for baptism learned to repeat the Lord's Prayer by memory.

Two = During the baptism services, the congregation prayed the Lord's Prayer.

Three = The Lord's Prayer was prayed during the Laying on of Hands (healing)
services.
Four = Clergy recited the Lord's Prayer at the beginning of the Eucharist.
Five = By omitting the phrase 'daily bread,' the Lord's Prayer was recited
during morning and evening prayer services.
Six = In the beginning, the Church of Rome opened each division of the mass
with the Lord's Prayer.

Misuse of the Lord's Prayer

- Little children have been, and are, taught the prayer without having been given explanations as to the prayer's words and intent.
- I believe it is safe to say that our Lord never expected to find His prayer used as part of the punishment/forgiveness cycle. Roman Catholics are used to hearing in the confessional, "As penance, say the Creed five times, and the Lord's Prayer five times."
- Overuse has reduced the Lord's Prayer to citations in a monotoned, bored, uninterested, unhearing, unfeeling worship 'duty.' This requirement in liturgy is important, but the prayer's presentation needs to be improved. Our Lord's Prayer needs to be spoken and received in the love and comfort it is meant to bring to its prayerers.

The Lord's Prayer in the Didache

The *Teaching of the Twelve Apostles* or *Didache* is a short church manual written in the middle of the second century. Popularly known as the 'Church Orders,' it is believed that parts of its oldest material probably go back to the first century, known as the 'Apostolic Times.'

It is thought that the *Didache's* Lord's Prayer originated in Syria around the time and place of the writing of the Gospel of Matthew, between 50 and 60 C.E. By the second century, the popular and highly needed *Didache* would be in every church in the surrounding areas.

Interestingly, the *Didache* utilized Matthew's version of the prayer in its church orders. The authors strongly believed that Matthew's work was more authentic.

It is strange to read about Matthew's work being more authentic when the *Didache* went ahead and made changes to the author's words. Supposedly, these changes are nothing more than an expression of freedom being allowed to new Christians. Maybe another way to say this is to point out what was covered earlier: uneven missionary training and separations over large land areas allows for differences in the teachings of Jesus's sermons. Bringing together groups of diverse people would have made it necessary to compromise and reconcile. The end goal was to produce cohesive writing like the 'church orders'. Following are three examples of where the *Didache* did not adhere strictly to Matthew's version.

One = Instead of 'as we also have forgiven our debtors,' the Didache states, 'as we also forgive our debtors.' The wording changes its meaning from past to present tense.

Two = Matthew's phrase of 'our debt' was changed to 'our debts' because it was (and is) believed that man is in a constant state of sinfulness rather than an occasional or regularly committed wrongdoing.

Three = A doxology was added to the prayer, though not the popular one in use today, 'For thine is the kingdom, and the power, and the glory, forever and ever. Amen.' The Didache used a short form of doxology that read: 'For thine is the power and the glory, forever.'

For all the writings about changes and uses, it is refreshing to know that, through the writings of antiquity, we still have Jesus's words, actions, and determined leadership to guide our way, our prayers

What Past Theologians Wrote Concerning Jesus's the Lord's Prayer

The Greek's pluralism philosophy was that man's nature pulled him toward a spiritual realm while exerting equal force toward an earthly life. Plato's philosophy included the belief that the duality of man's existence is a life-long condition from which there is no escape. In other words, the secular versus the sacred.

Jesus disputed Plato's philosophy by pointing out that all the earth and humankind belong to God, with God. Under our Lord's guidance, especially under the influence of New Life's encouragement, man is made whole by giving us purpose rather than mere random existence.

The Lord's Prayer reflects this wholeness by speaking of God's Kingdom as being present. Our 'daily bread' is a source of daily physical and spiritual nourishment. Upon our asking, sins are forgiven. In following our Lord's request, we forgive others' sins and thus are able to live in harmony with them. The Will of our Father is a daily goal strived for, as doing Father's Will offers personal satisfaction, brought about by a thoughtful understanding that we are a participant in helping bring together Heaven and Earth.

The prayer offers—in how the words come together, how the phrases flow evenly and spiritually throughout, an orderly construction, and a rhythmic nature to join cohesively—the perfect prayer. We have discussed other prayers and have seen that they begin with humans and their problems, and somewhere near the end, the prayer gets to godly concerns. The Lord's Prayer has taught us to put our Father first. Our needs come a distant second. We start with Heaven and slowly return to Earth.

Have you ever noticed that by the time we are finished with praising our Father and thinking about the many gifts and blessings we have received, that the earthly concerns are not nearly as important? Our problems fall into a healthier perspective. First, we know that Father will give us an answer on what is needed to resolve the issue. Second, we have come to understand that our timetable is not God's timetable. Often, if we leave things alone, the situation straightens out. It can be a miracle the way an answer is given!

Not surprising, the Primitive Church's name for prayer was 'eucharistia.' The term means 'thanksgiving.' When considering the Lord's Prayer, we begin to see how prayer is, from beginning to end, a form of thank. As we contemplate Jesus's insightful words into our human condition, we begin to experience comfort in the knowledge that we can leave situations in His hand, we can submit to His will without losing anything of our essence. Instead, we gain.

Church Father Origen was the most important theologian and biblical scholar of the early Greek Church. Origen wrote in his thesis on prayer that all proper prayer would consist of five elements: Praise—Thanksgiving—Confession—Petition—Praise. He purported that, without deviation, all the components must be precisely in this order. One would think the Lord's Prayer would have met with his approval. However, as you will soon read, this was not the observation he made about Jesus's prayer.

The Lord's Prayer has been studied, scrutinized, taken apart, and put back together. It has been written about, sermonized, and talked about in the media. People request its reading on their special occasions. Relatives want to hear the prayer when at a wake, at the gravesite, or during a memorial service. Of all of Jesus's set of words, like with the Beatitudes, the Lord's Prayer is the one most remembered, most requested, and most prayed.

Following is what famed religious thinkers wrote about the Lord's Prayer.

THEOLOGIAN	COMMENT
Tertullian (cl45–200)	Called the Lord's Prayer a 'new outline of prayer,' and referred to it as, "The epitome of the whole Gospel."
Cyprian (c200–258)	Referred to the Lord's Prayer as both a public and private (common) prayer.
Origen (cl85–c254)	Said in his work On Prayer that the Lord's Prayer was an outline or a sketch. Maybe one reason he thought this is that the prayer opens with praise, but the Roman Catholic Church has never included a doxology to the prayer's ending, so there is no ending praise.
Cyril of Jerusalem (c315–c386)	Between the Passion and Easter seasons in 350, he delivered a series of 'mystagogic catecheses' (mysteries within Catholicism, such as the Sacraments of Baptism, Confirmation, and the Eucharist). In the fifth one, he explained the role the Lord's Prayer plays in the liturgy of the mass.
Saint Augustine (354–430)	Emphasized that the petition for forgiveness was the most important one of all. He also said, "We need to use words (when we pray) to remind ourselves to consider what we are asking." (en.wikipedia.org)

Meister Eckhard (cl260–1327)	A mystic who said that "The most powerful form of prayer is the prayer of a person who is not obsessed with particular forms of prayer." (eckhartsociety.org) Standardized prayers were, therefore, 'not conducive to a free mind.'
Thomas Aquinas (c1225–1274)	He wrote 'Catechetical Instructions,' wherein he spoke to the five qualities of the Lord's Prayer and 'A Short Explanation of the Whole Prayer.' His five questions were that prayer must be confident, ordered, suitable, devout, and humble. In his Explanation, Aquinas states that the prayer "contains all that we ought to desire and all that we ought to avoid." (ourcatholicprayers.com/acquinas)
Martin Luther (1483–1546)	Stated that, "the Lord's Prayer is the highest, noblest, and best prayer."
John Wesley (1703–1791)	Wrote that Jesus had, "Dictated to us a most perfect and universal form of prayer. It comprehends all our real wants, expresses all our lawful desires—a complete directory and full exercise of all our devotions." (soulshepherding.org)

Jean Carmignac (1914–1986)	In 1965, he published an article, "Fais que nous n 'entrionspas dans la tentation" in Revue Biblique 72, pp 218–226, where his rendered version of the sixth petition caused a sensation when he pointed out that in the Hebrew language, a negative before a causative verb creates two possible meanings; either 'causes us not to come' or 'do not cause us to come.' So confused, and full of ambiguity, Carmignac implied in the following year, that 'God would submit us to temptation if we did not pray to him not to.' (jstor.org) His writing brings us into a full appreciation of the difficulties of translation. In 1969, he published 'Recherches sur le 'Notre Pete' which is 608 pages long, with 80 pages of bibliographies on the Lord's Prayer. It is one of the most comprehensive examinations of the prayer, but he considered it an unfinished work! Carmignac argued that Jesus spoke the prayer in Hebrew, which caused many scholars to rethink their position on the issue.

Reflections from Your Author
Part One – The Questions

As a final ending to this book, allow me to share the frustration of reading works by authors who get hooked on debating a premise which dilutes what Jesus and Christianity are about; that is, a New Life. Questions are noble, healthy motivators toward learning but not when redundantly made into themes that become an entity unto themselves. This neither aids in spiritual growth nor helps in the daily Christian life. How many of the theological arguments and debates are geared toward the laity? Or were they never meant to be heard by them? In these dialogues, should not the result be to bring about a more in-depth understanding, or greater clarity to the worshipping people?

Jesus's lineage, birthplace, birth date, Son of God/Son of Man twisters, good/bad relationship with family, education, trade, and the purpose(s) of women followers, have all been brought into question millions of times. Questions led to centuries of research. Where are the answers, the higher degree of understanding? We continue to experience the same puzzling issues:

- The wisdom in choosing the 'original twelve' (including Judas Iscariot).
- The fact that Jesus quoted volumes from the Old Testament and other resources.
- The open suggestions that Gospel writers changed history, altered facts, stretched truths so that Jesus's life would correlate with ancient prophecies.
- The issues of pre-Easter or post-Easter writings continue to be brought into question.

- Topical questions that never cease, never have universal satisfactory answers, such as: the years of ministry—the timing and places of events—miracle scrutiny—did Jesus believe in Satan debates—healing explanations—psychosomatic illness—trauma reduction—mass hysteria—autosuggestion—and, of course, the devil-sin-sickness triad.
- Doubts that 5,000 person received food, the necessity of baptism, and asking Father to 'forgive us our sins' from a supposedly sinless man have all been brought into question.
- The debate about who killed Jesus: secular or sacred? Or what killed Jesus: religious or political? Or if Jesus took a drug to ease His pain while hanging on the cross? His empty tomb—was this temporary, or His body removed by loyal followers?

One event not questioned—the one occurrence that writers, researchers, religious scholars all seem to be in awe of—is the undisputed fact that SOMETHING occurred after the crucifixion. That 'something' turned Apostles, Disciples, Followers, and family members into such staunch believers that many endured painful, tortured deaths with the name of 'Jesus' on their lips.

From out of the trade of mostly fishermen, an accountant, a horse breeder, a student religious scholar, and a couple of Zealots, this highly mixed group produced one of the world's most influential religion. It continues in strength for, even after 2,000 years, people worldwide are still willing to die in His name.

Logically, psychologically, spiritually, we cannot deny that some event happened after the crucifixion. A new Faith, our Christian New Life—a happening so strong, so powerful, that it pulled the scattered, frightened Followers back together into a forceful, brilliant, unto-death-committed group of Believers. Included are Jesus's family members who had rejected both the teachings of Jesus and His claim of messiahship up to the time of the Resurrection.

What pulled these frightened, running, practically ex-followers, doubters at-the-cross, back together? Our resurrected Christ! The One who walked, talked, and ate among the people—after His death!

So, ask about any aspect of the life of Jesus. Questions are meaningful because questions stimulate thinking, motivate researchers, and open previously closed hearts, minds, and doors. Questions encourage information exchange and promote growth. Fundamentally, questions deepen Faith. Seeking answers can help us to get a handle on our Christian religion. To ask questions and find 'truth' and 'fact' about yesteryears' events are wholesome, informative, and exciting endeavors. But let us not err in getting 'hung up' on any one aspect of it. Not when we are faced today with the critical issues of survival.

And while questions will continue, let us remember this one indisputable fact:

'Heaven and earth will pass away
but my words will not pass away.'
Matthew 24:35 and Mark 13:31

Part Two – The Answers

In the introduction, I wrote, 'From the soul to the brain to the heart run the circular threads of longing. We crave what God craves. Spiritual steppingstones lead the way.' The finishing thought here is that Our Lord's Prayer does this when we stop to listen to the Will of our Father. Then we make the necessary response.

Herein lies a huge problem: Humans love their freewill and see where sharing this Will—even with our Creator—is a 'giving in' or a 'giving up' of a personal right. It is a choice.

It sounds as though I am getting into mysticism when I say that in the prayerful sharing of wills, I receive back clarity of purpose that enlightens and strengthens personal direction. The lucidity is a most humbling experience, becoming precious, and something that I must carry out rightly. Clarity is a responsibility. I become a better person because I discover anger, sarcasm, and negativity places me emotionally and spiritually where I do not want to be. Acting on these emotions cloud the clarity. I cannot dishonor this gift. I could never ignore the pleasure it gives my soul.

This divine offering is available to every individual on Earth. Trust me. I am not special, nor am I unique. And this is not false pride talking. My limitations and flaws are many. If there is such a thing as 'too human,' well, that would be my category. That is how I know that this divine offering is available to you and everyone.

My prayer is that you, at this moment, are asking yourself, "How do I get there? How do I go about—not giving up my Will—but sharing it?"

So, I say to you, my reader: find a quiet place. Be still. Close your eyes.

Pray aloud, 'Our'

And think of all those whom you know.

Those you do not know.

Those you would like to know, and why you would like to know them.

Now think about Jesus. The first time, not your random thoughts, but this: Jesus of Palestine. In the beginning of writing this book, I invited a person to read the first chapter. It was quickly returned to me. The 'Jewishness' of Jesus was upsetting. Marlene Brickmeier, one of the books' readers, comes from a Jewish background and recently wrote me this note: 'The roots of Christianity began with Jesus's ministry, yet it is a curious thought as to why some Christians forget that Jesus was Jewish. His holiness and ministry derived from Hebrew teachings. He was born Jewish, grew up Jewish, lived Jewish, and preached and died Jewish. Without His Jewishness, would Jesus have taught His disciples the Lord's Prayer?' Her insightful words make for an excellent question, one that deserves consideration from every Christian.

So, in this first step of connecting your Will with our Father's, think about Jesus's first-century life, about how the Hebrew religious structure, Palestine's turmoil, and the humble people's miserable lives all provided the golden opportunity for ministry. What comes to mind is the term 'perfect.' Springing to mind is how our Father provides the perfect person to be in the perfect situation at the perfect time. Jesus's 'I will follow You' baptism aligned Father's and Jesus's Wills into perfection for the Earth's salvation.

Pray aloud 'Father'

And think of how it feels to be loved unconditionally.

Think of how it will feel to be in Father's love for all eternity, where souls live without pain, with purpose, where peace and joy bloom in every hour. Contemplate what you might be able to do in your life to help bring about these feelings now. There is no future like the present!

Pray aloud 'who art in heaven'

And think about what Heaven looks like, feels like.

What will it be like living in Heaven?

Who is in Heaven with you? Can you see them? Feel them?

Who else do you want to be in Heaven with you? Will they be? Is there anything you can do to help them be on the path to Heaven?

Pray aloud 'Hallowed'

And think about your very first meeting with Father. How 'hallowed' was the sight? How 'hallowed' were the first sentences?

Think of being in total awe.

Have you had this experience as a person?

Did anything later happen that changed the feeling?

Can you see where your awe of the 'hallowedness' of Father is different than what you could ever feel about another human being?

Pray aloud 'be thy Name'

And think about what is in a name. Does a name influence or ordain behavior? One's destiny? Does a feeling about someone cause a higher or lower opinion of his or her name?

When you pray 'Father,' 'Heaven,' 'Hallowed,' and 'Name' together, does a difference in feeling and thinking occur?

Pray aloud 'thy Kingdom'

And picture how Heaven's Kingdom looks.

What is its appeal?

How is it different than what you have right now?

Is there anything you can do now or soon, which will help you have a life a bit more like what you believe God's Kingdom is like?

Pray aloud 'Come'

And ask yourself why you want 'thy Kingdom come.'

Is this an accurate statement?

If this statement is how you feel, how would it change your present circumstances?

Pray aloud 'your will be done'

And ask yourself what kind of 'Will' do you believe Father wants 'done' right now?

Do you see any possibility of that happening anytime soon?

Pray aloud 'on Earth as it is in heaven'

And when you answered the above question, do you see now how your answer might have been different if you had considered Earth and Heaven connection first?

What do you think Father's Will is for the Earth?

Mentally list what you would love to see done as Father's Will here on Earth.

<u>Pray aloud 'And forgive me and others our sins.'</u>

Think of the mercy given when, with every 'I am sorry for…

'Please forgive me' and your slate is wiped clean. The sin disappears from Father's memory, never to be thought of again. Your soul returns to its original snowy whiteness.

Now think how great it would be if you could forget about the sin. Think about how great it would be if you could forgive yourself over this sin.

Pray aloud, 'As we also have forgiven those who have sinned against us.'

Is this the truth? Have you forgiven everyone who has ever sinned against you?

Consider this: do you think you could say to Father that you have forgiven everyone except for_____

because_____

and then explain the reason(s) for the difficulty you are having in making the forgiveness total?

_____

_____

Do you think your loving Father in Heaven understands your need for more time?

Will your request be granted? Do you believe a time limit is involved?

<u>Pray aloud 'And do not bring us to the time of trial.'</u>

You do not want any more problems. Take a moment to think about your problem.

Consider the ways you might try to resolve your problem. Are you looking at all sides?

Are you thinking of what damage could occur if you do not act, do not solve, do not refuse?

Will it be better to act or to do nothing? Or call in someone to help you work the problem through?

You do not want any more temptations in your life. Take a moment to consider what does tempt you.

Consider how strong you are right now to resist temptation. What steps can you take to increase your strength?

<u>Pray aloud 'But rescue us from evil.'</u>

What does evil look like to you?

Do you have evil in your life?

Do you realize that you must rid your life of evil? If necessary, get the help you need. Fighting evil is not something one should try on one's own.

<u>Pray aloud 'Amen.'</u>

There had been no 'amen' on the ending of the Lord's Prayer because it is not included in the Gospel's renderings. Today, we have the term and pray it in our prayer closing. 'Amen' means 'so be it.' Is this not a fantastic term?

Go back over all the statements you just made and add an 'amen' to them.

Observe how it changes and emphasizes your thoughts and feelings. That finishing touch helps bring closer.

I shared this exercise with you to show its importance in my life. Events in my life had been helped by an intense concentration upon one or two phrases, depending upon the circumstance.

I held on to the phrase needed when suffering through childhood abandonment, a rape, a beating, operations, anger issues, a stubborn act of refusal to offer forgiveness, an obstinate 'my will, not yours,' an immovable lack of compassion, and the long list goes on.

Looking back on this autobiography, I see a refusal to grow into a spiritual being. Instead of seeing a gain into the essence of who I am or will become, I saw only who I was at that present moment. Self-satisfaction, pride, and anger were my enemies, my evils, and my downfall.

Do not be foolish like I was. Save yourself decades of struggle. Invite Jesus, His New Life, and His salvation into your life. You and your life will be changed—not all at once—but gradually and permanently. You will be so thankful, and I am not referring to the promise of life everlasting, but the promise of an earthly life filled with purpose. You will become a conduit between Heaven and Earth. You will be a representative of the attributes of the Christian life. You are the one people will look to when seeking the justice and mercy needed in this world of ours today. This is a responsibility that you are more than capable of filling. I know this because you would not have picked up this book and studied it if you were not already following the Will of our Father.

Do not stop here. Continue with your search, asking the questions, finding your answers. Ask Jesus to be your Guide, the Holy Spirit for protection, and for our Father's counsel as you seek His will. May your journey be truly blessed.

LIVING IS FOR NOW
ETERNITY IS FOREVER

Bibliography Listing

ABBA! FATHER! By Rev. Carey Landry; Choral Music; Epoch Universal Publications; unknown state and year.

ABBA! FATHER! By V. R. Schreiber; Augsburg Publishing House; Minneapolis; 1988.

ABBA – MEDITATIONS BASED ON THE LORD'S PRAYER by Evelyn Underhill; Forward Movements Pub.; Ohio; reprinted 1982.

A HISTORY OF THE JEWISH PEOPLE IN THE TIME OF JESUS CHRIST, First Division, Volume II; by Emil Schurer, translated by Rev. John MacPherson; Hendrickson Publishers; Peabody MA; nineth edition, July 2014.

AND STILL IS OURS TODAY by Father F. Washington Jarvis; Seabury Press; NY; 1980.

ARCHAEOLOGY, HISTORY, AND SOCIETY IN GALILEE by Richard A.

Horsley; Trinity Press International; Harrisburg PA; 1996.

AND STILL IS OURS TODAY by A.W. Pink; Baker Book House, Michigan; 1982.

BEATITUDES & THE LORD'S PRAYER FOR EVERYMAN, THE by Dr. William Barclay; Harper & Row, New York; 1964.

BEHOLD THE MAN edited by Ralph L. Woods; MacMillian Co.; New York; 1944.

BIBLE HAS THE ANSWER, THE by Henry M. Morris; Baker Book House; Grand Rapids, Michigan; 1971.

BOOK OF COMMON PRAYER THE, According to the use of the Episcopal Church; The Church Hymnal Corporation; NY; 1984.

BOOK OF JEWISH KNOWLEDGE by Nathan Ausubel; Crown Publishers Inc.; NY; 1964.

BOOK OF MORMON, THE, translated by Joseph Smith, Jun.; The Church of Jesus Christ of Latter-day Saints; Utah; 1982.

BREAD BROKEN AND SHARED by Father Paul Bernier; Ava Maria Press; IN; 1981.

BREAK-THROUGH by Tom Rees; Word Books; Texas; 1970.

CHRISTIAN ETHICS by Georgia Harkness; Abingdon Press; New York; 1952.

CHRISTIAN SANCTIFIED BY THE LORD'S PRAYER, THE by John Nicholas Group, S.J.; (translated from a French Unpublished Manuscript); Burns Oates & Washbourne Ltd. (official Publishers to the Holy See); London; 1930.

COLUMBIA VIKING DESK ENCYCLOPEDIA, THE, Vol. 2; compiled and edited at Columbia University; Viking Press; New York; 1953.

CREED OF CHRIST, THE by Gerald Heard; The Religious Book Club; London; 1944.

DICTIONARY OF BEHAVIORAL SCIENCE edited by Benjamin B. Wolman; Van Nostrand Reinhold Co.; New York; 1973.

DICTIONARY OF BIBLE & RELIGION, THE, by William H. Gentz, General Editor; Abindon Press; Tenn.; 1986.

DICTIONARY OF BIBLICAL THEOLOGY edited by Xavier Leon-Dufour; The Seabury Press, New York; 1973.

DIFFICULT SAYINGS OF JESUS, THE, by Father William Neil; Wm. B. Eerdmans Pub. Co.; Grand Rapids; 1975.

DIVINE COMEDY OF DANTE ALIGHIERI, THE, The Carlyle-Wicksteed Translation; Random House, Inc.; New York; 1950.

EDUCATION FOR MINISTRY (Four Year Program with Vols. I–IV) from The School of Theology, The University of the South; Sewanee, Tenn.; 1986.

ELEMENTS OF THE SPIRITUAL LIFE, THE by F. P. Harton, B.D.; S.P.C.K.; London; 1957.

ENCYCLOPEDIA AMERICANA, INTERNATIONAL EDITION, THE; Grolier, Inc.; Conn. 1990.

ENCYCLOAEDIA BRITANNICA, CD 97', Encyclopedia Britannica, Inc.; Chicago IL; 1997.

ENCYCLOPEDIA OF HUMAN BEHAVIOR, THE, vol. 1, by Robert M. Golderson, Ph.D.; Doubleday & Co., Inc.; New York; 1970.

ESSAYS IN HONOR OF JOSEPH P. BRENNAN edited by Robert F. McNamara; Saint Bernard's Seminary; New York; 1976.

FAITHS MEN LIVE BY, THE by Charles F. Potter; Prentice-Hall, Inc.; New York; 1954.

FAMILY DEVOTIONAL BIBLE (Authorized or King James Version); De Vore & Sons, Inc.; Kansas; 1960.

FIFTY KEY WORDS: THE BIBLE by Julian Charley; John Knox Press; Virginia; 1971.

FIVE BOOKS OF MOSES, THE; edited by Everett Fox; The Schocken Bible: Volume 1; Schocken Books, NY, NY; 1995.

FOUR PORTRAITS, ONE JESUS – A Survey of Jesus and the Gospels by Mark L. Strauss; Zondervan; Grand Rapid MI; 2007.

FREEDOM OF SIMPLICITY by Dr. Richard J. Foster; Harper & Row Publishers; San Francisco CA; 1981.

GATES OF PRAYER – THE NEW UNION PRAYERBOOK by the Central Conference of American Rabbis; New York; eleventh printing, 1987.

GIVERS AND THE TAKERS, THE by Cris Evatt & Bruce Feld; Macmillan Publishing Co., Inc.; New York; 1983.

GOD CALLING edited by A. J. Russell; Barbour & Co., Inc.; New Jersey; 1985.

GOD'S PSYCHIATRY by Charles L. Allen; Fleming H. Revell Co.; New Jersey; 1953.

GOOD NEWS FOR MODERN MAN, American Bible Society; New York; 1966.

GREAT EVENTS OF BIBLE TIMES edited by Dr. B. M. Metzger, Dr. D.

Goldstein & J. Ferguson, MA, BD; Doubleday & Co., Inc.; New York; 1987.

HARD SAYINGS OF JESUS by F. F. Bruce; InterVarsity Press; Downers Grove, IL; 1983.

HARPER'S BIBLE DICTIONARY, general editor Paul J. Achtemeier; Harper & Row; San Francisco, CA; 1985.

HARPER'S ENCYCLOPEDIA OF BIBLE LIFE by Madeleine S. and J. Lane Miller; Harper & Row; Edison NJ; 1978.

HOLY BIBLE, KING JAMES VERSION; Zondervan Publishing House; Grand Rapids, Michigan; 1994.

HOLY BIBLE, NEW REVISED STANDARD VERSION; The New Oxford Annotated Bible with the Apocrypha; edited by Bruce M. Metzger and Roland E. Murphy; Oxford University Press; NY, NY; 1989.

HOLY BIBLE, NEW AMERICAN STANDARD BIBLE; Ryrie Study Bible; Charles Caldwell Ryrie; Moody Publishers; Chicago IL; 1995 update.

HOLMAN ILLUSTRATED BIBLE DICTIONARY, General Editor T. C. Butler; Holman Reference; Nashville TN; 2003.

HYMNAL, THE 1982, according to the use of the Episcopal Church; The Church Hymnal Corp.; New York; 1985.

I'M OK – YOU'RE OK by Dr. Thomas A. Harris; Harper & Row; New York; 1969.

INHERIT THE PROMISE by Pierson Parker; The Seabury Press; Conn.; 1957.

INTERNATIONAL BIBLE COMMENTARY, THE, editor William R. Farmer; The Liturgical Press; Collegeville, MN; 1998.

INTERPRETER'S DICTIONARY OF THE BIBLE, THE, in Four Volumes; Abingdon Press; New York; 1962.

INTERPRETER'S DICTIONARY OF THE BIBLE, THE, Supplementary Volume;

Abingdon Press; Nashville, Tenn.; 1976.

JAMES, THE BROTHER OF JESUS – The Key to Unlocking the Secrets of Early Christianity and the Dead Sea Scrolls by Robert Eisenman; Penguin Books; NY, NY; 1998.

JESUS AND THE VICTORY OF GOD by N. T. Wright; Fortress Press, MN; 1996.

JESUS BOOK, THE, paraphrased by Ken Taylor; Hodder and Stoughton and Coverdale House Pub.; London; 1972.

JESUS' JEWISHNESS, edited by James H. Charlesworth; The American Interfaith Institute; Crossroad; New York; 1991.

JESUS NOW by Leslie F. Brandt; Concordia Pub. House; St. Louis, Missouri; 1978.

THE JEWISH STUDY BIBLE, a TANAKH Translation, editors Adele Berlin and Marc Zvi Brettler; Jewish Publication Society; Oxford University Press; NY, NY; 1999.

JEWS AND CHRISTIANS, edited by James H. Charlesworth; Crossroad; NY; 1990.

JUDAISM, volumes 1–2; by George Foot Moore; Hendrickson Publishers; Peabody MA; 1997.

KEY OF HEAVEN, THE, Imprimatur: Er. Jos. Carton De Wiart, vic. gen., 1939; Nihil Obstat.: Arthur J. Scanlan, S.T.D., Censor Librorum; Imprimatur: Patrick Cardinal Hayes, Archbishop, N.Y., 1924; The Regina Press; New York.

KING JAMES BIBLE, Holman Pronouncing Addition; PA; 1925.

LAYMAN LOOKS AT THE LORD'S PRAYER, A, by W. Phillip Keller, Moody Press, Chicago; 1976.

'LEAD US NOT INTO TEMPTATION' by Dr. Peter S. Cameron; New College; Edinburgh; article in The Expository Times, v101, p299–301; July, 1990.

LET YOUR KINGDOM COME by Watch Tower Bible & Tract Society of Pennsylvania; Watchtower Bible & Tract Society of New York, Inc. and International Bible Students Assoc., New York; 1981.

LIFE OF CHRIST by Bishop Fulton J. Sheen; McGraw-Hill Book Co., Inc.; NY; 1960.

LIFE OF CHRIST, THE, by Andres Fernandez, S.J.; Translation by Paul Barrett, O.F.M.Cap.; Newman Press; Westminster, MD.; Second Printing 1959.

LION ENCYCLOPEDIA OF THE BIBLE, THE, edited by Pat Alexander; Reader's Digest Assoc., Inc.; New York; 1987.

LIVING THE LORD'S PRAYER by Everett L. Fullam with Bob Slosser; Chosen Books, Virginia; 1980.

LIVING THE LORD'S PRAYER by Dr. Carroll E. Simcox; Morehouse-Gorham Co., New York; 1955.

LORD'S PRAYER (LUKE 11.2–4) IN THE HISTORIC ENGLISH VERSIONS, THE, paper received from The Rev. James Kelly of the Southwest Diocese, Florida.

LORD'S PRAYER, THE by The Rev. Dr. Peter H. Davids; The Brotherhood of St. Andrew, Inc.; unknown state and date.

LORD'S PRAYER, THE, by St. Cyprian of Carthage; translated by Edmond Bonin; Christian Classics; Maryland; 1983.

LORD'S PRAYER, THE, by E. F. Scott, D.D.; Charles Scribner's Sons; New York; 1951.

LORD'S PRAYER, THE by F. J. Sheed; The Seabury Press Inc.; New York; 1975.

LORD'S PRAYER & JEWISH LITURGY, THE, edited by Jakob J. Petuchowski and Michael Brocke; The Seabury Press; N.Y.; 1978.

LORD'S PRAYER IN ITS BIBLICAL SETTING, THE, by Charles M. Laymon, S.T.B. & Th.D.; Abingdon Press; New York; 1968.

LORD'S PRAYER IN THE EARLY CHURCH, THE, by Frederic Henry Chase, B.D.; Cambridge at the University Press; London; 1891.

MAN FROM GALILEE, THE: A LIFE OF JESUS by Dr. George M. Lamsa; Doubleday & Co., Inc., New York; 1970.

MAN FROM NAZARETH, THE, by Harry Emerson Fosdick; Harper & Brothers; New York; 1949.

MAN WHO CHANGED THE WORLD, THE, vol. 1 by Dr. Herbert Lockyer; Zondervan Publishing House; Michigan; 1966.

MIND OF JESUS, THE by William Barclay; HarperSanFrancisco, NY, NY; paperback edition, 1976.

MYSTERIES OF THE BIBLE, editors of The Reader's Digest Association, Inc.; NY; 1988.

MYSTERY MISSION OF SALVATION IN CHRIST JESUS, THE: Birth, Mission, Death, and Resurrection by Dr. Ibim Alfred; Author House UK; Bloomington IN; 2017.

NEW ENCYCLOPEDIA BRITANNICA, THE, by the editors of Britannica, Inc.; IL; 1987.

NEW ENGLISH BIBLE, THE, Oxford University Press & Cambridge University Press; England; 1961.

NEW OXFORD ANNOTATED BIBLE WITH THE APOCRYPHA THE, EXPANDED EDITION (an Ecumenical Study Bible) edited by Herbert G. May & Bruce M. Metzger; Oxford University Press, Inc.; New York; 1977.

NEW WESTMINSTER DICTIONARY OF THE BIBLE, THE, edited by Henry Snyder Gehman; The Westminster Press; Philadelphia, Penn.; 1970.

OLD TESTAMENT, THE – AN INTRODUCTION by Rolf Rendtorff; Fortress Press; Philadelphia PA; 1991.

OLD TESTAMENT PSEUDEPIGRAPHA, THE, volume 2, by James H. Charlesworth, editor; The Anchor Bible Reference Library; Doubleday; NY, NY; 1985.

ON PRAYER by Karl Rahner, S.J.; Paulist Press Deus Books; New York; 1968.

OTHER BIBLE, THE edited by Willis Barnstone; HarperCollins; San Francisco CA; 1984.

OUR LIFE OF PRAYER by Rev. J. Wilson Sutton; Morehouse-Gorham Co.; NY; 1938.

OXFORD AMERICAN PRAYER BOOK COMMENTARY, THE by Massey H. Shepherd, Jr.; fifth printing, Oxford University Press; New York; 1955.

PERSON REBORN, THE by Paul Tournier, and translated by Edwin Hudson; Harper & Row; New York; 1966.

POCKET PRAYER BOOK, THE, Otto L. Garcia, J.C.D., Diocesan Censor and Francis J. Mugavero, D.D., Bishop of Brooklyn, NY; The Regina Press; Belgium; 1981.

POWERHOUSE OF PRAYER, A; Anglican Fellowship of Prayer; Florida; year unknown.

PRAYER by Karl Barth; Second Edition; edited by Don E. Saliers from the translation of Sara F. Terrien; The Westminster Press; Philadelphia, Pennsylvania; 1985.

PRAYER CAN CHANGE YOUR LIFE by William R. Parker and Elaine St. Johns; Guideposts; New York; 1957.

PRAYER THAT TEACHES TO PRAY, THE, by Marcus Dods, D.D. (1834–1909); Hodder and Stoughton; London; no publishing date of book given.

PRAYER WEAPONS by Allegra Harrah; Fleming H. Revell Co.; New Jersey; 1976. READER'S DIGEST BIBLE, THE, The Reader's Digest Assoc.; New York; 1982. RELIGIONS OF THE WORLD by Gerald L. Berry; Barnes & Noble, Inc.; New York; 1956.

SAVING PARADISE by Rita N. Brock and Rebecca A. Parker; Beacon Press; Boston MA; 2008.

SENSE AND NONSENSE ABOUT PRAYER by Lehman Strauss; Moody Press; Chicago, IL; 1974.

SEVEN SAYINGS OF THE SAVIOUR ON THE CROSS, THE by Arthur W. Pink; Baker Book House, Michigan; 1958.

SHIPS THAT PASS IN THE NIGHT by Beatrice Harraden; G. Munro; New York; 1894.

SINS OF THE DAY by Longmans, Green and Co.; New York; 1959.

SITTING AT THE FEET OF JESUS by Ann Spangler and Lois Tverberg; Zondervan; Grand Rapids, MI; 2009.

SKETCHES OF JEWISH SOCIAL LIFE by Alfred Edersheim; Hendrickson Publishers; Peabody MA; 1994.

SOCIAL WORLD OF LUKE-ACTS, THE edited by Jerome H. Neyrey; Hendrickson Publishers; Peabody, Massachusetts; 1991.

STRONG'S EXHAUSTIVE CONCORDANCE OF THE BIBLE by James Strong; Hendrickson Publishers; Peabody, Massachusetts; sixth printing, 2014.

TABERNACLE OF MOSES, THE by Kevin J. Conner; City Christian Publishing, Portland OR; 1976.

TANAKH TRANSLATION of the JEWISH STUDY BIBLE – including the Works of the TORAH, NEVI'IM, KETHUVIM; editors Adele Berlin and Marc Zvi Brettler with consulting editor Michael Fishband; Oxford University Press; Oxford NY; 1999.

TEN GREAT RELIGIONS by James Freeman Clarke; The Riverside Press; Cambridge, MA; 1890.

THEY TEACH US TO PRAY by Reginald E.O. White; Harper & Brothers; NY; 1957.

THOUGHTS ON THE LORD'S PRAYER by Elizabeth Wordsworth (Principal of Lady Margaret Hall, Oxford); Longmans, Green, & Co.; New York and Bombay; 1898.

TO MAKE INTERCESSION by Sibyl Harton; Hodder & Stoughton; London; 1964.

TWICE SEVEN WORDS by Agnes Sanford; Logos, International; New Jersey; 1971. UNDERSTANDING THE LORD'S PRAYER by Philip B. Harner; Fortress Press; PA; 1975.

WANDERINGS – History of the Jews by Chaim Potok; Fawcett Crest; NY, NY; 1980.

WE DARE TO SAY OUR FATHER by Louis Evely; Herder & Herder, New York; 2nd edition 1967.

WEBSTER'S NEW UNIVERSAL UNABRIDGED DICTIONARY, Second Edition; New World Dictionaries, Simon and Schuster; New York; 1983.

WEBSTER'S SEVENTH NEW COLLEGIATE DICTIONARY, by the editors of the G. & C. Merriam Co., Massachusetts; 1976.

WHERE IS GOD IN MY SUFFERING? by Dr. Daniel J. Simundson; Augsburg Publishing House; Minn.; 1983.

"WHO DO MEN SAY THAT I AM?" by Cullen Murphy, The Atlantic Magazine; 1986.

WHO'S WHO IN THE BIBLE (Old Testament, Apocrypha, and New Testament) by Joan Comay and Ronald Brownrigg; Bonanza Books; New York; 1980.

WORLD ALMANAC & BOOK OF FACTS 1991, THE, by the editors of World Almanac; Pharos Books; Scripps Howard Co.; New York; 1990.

WORLD'S LIVING RELIGIONS, THE by Robert Ernest Hume; Charles Scribner's Sons; NY, NY; 1950.

ZONDERVAN NIV EXHAUSTIVE CONCORDANCE; editors E. W. Goodrick, J. R. Kohlenberger III, and J. A. Swanson; Zondervan Publishing House; Grand Rapid MI; s.e. 1999.

Internet Sources

www.academia<updates@academia-mail.com

www.bartleby.com

www.biblegateway.com

www.biblehub.com

www.bibleinfo.com

www.biblestudy.org

www.bitstream.org https://blogs.ancientfaith.com

www.blueletterbible.org

www.britannica.com

www.christiananswers.net

www.christianity.stackexchange.com

www.christianitytoday.com

www.cjh.org (5,000 years of Jewish history)

www.eckhartsoiety.org

www.en.wikipedia.org

www.francisanmedia.org

www.gotquestions.org

www.jewishvirtuallibrary.org

www.jewsforjesus.org

www.jstor.org

www.myjewishlearning.com

www.newadvent.org

www.ourcatholicprayers.com/acquinas

www.ruachisrael.com (MessianicJudaism)

www.sociologydiscussion.com

www.soulshepherding.org

www.torahmates.org

www.truthonlybible.org

www.worldjewishcongress.org
www.yivoencyclopedia.org.jewish/encyclopedia

CPSIA information can be obtained
at www.ICGtesting.com
Printed in the USA
BVHW031226091222
653840BV00004B/153